HD58.8 .Z548 2010
Business restructuring :an action
template for reducing cost and growi
33663004702862

Business Restructuring

Business Restructuring

An Action Template for Reducing Cost and Growing Profit

Carla Zilka

WILEY

John Wiley & Sons, Inc.

Published by John Wiley & Sons, Inc., Hoboken, New Jersey.

Published simultaneously in Canada.

For general information on our other products and services, or technical support, please contact our Customer Care Department within the United States at 800-762-2974, outside the United States at 317-572-3993 or fax 317-572-4002.

Wiley also publishes its books in a variety of electronic formats. Some content that appears in print may not be available in electronic books.

For more information about Wiley products, visit our Web site at www.wiley.com.

Library of Congress Cataloging-in-Publication Data

Zilka, Carla
    Business restructuring : an action template for reducing cost and growing profit / Carla Zilka.
        p.   cm.
    Includes index.
    ISBN 978-0-470-50368-3
        1. Corporate reorganizations. 2.   Reengineering (Management)
    3. Organizational change—Management. I. Title.
    HD58.8.Z548 2010
    658.4'06—dc22
                                                        2009025217

Printed in the United States of America

*To my parents, Jenny and Carl Zilka, who always told me
I could do anything I put my mind to, and to stand
up for what I believe, no matter how difficult it may be.*

Contents

Foreword

A s Chairman and Chief Executive Officer of an investment brokerage firm involved in the equity capital markets, I am acutely aware that Wall Street, and companies in general, are in trouble. For most firms, revenue is slumping and profits are nonexistent. In my industry, brokers and brokerage firms are exiting the business at a record pace. There are many reasons why firms and individuals fail, but one thing is certain: There is no such thing as "Business as usual" on Wall Street. The brokerage industry has changed more during the past several years than it has changed over the last quarter century. Although my firm, FTN Equity Capital Markets, is one of the most well-respected research firms on Wall Street, having a high-quality product is no guarantee of success.

Running a small firm such as ours, or any small-to midsized company, does not provide management with the luxury of hiring and retaining a consulting firm at a time when profitability is under pressure. Still, management must adapt to this rapidly changing environment and both restructure existing businesses to match the paradigm shifts in the marketplace and simultaneously develop new businesses and strategies to leverage core competencies. Ultimately these adaptations will decide whether companies such as ours survive. From personal experience, adapting is no small task. The market is increasingly creating winners and losers . . . and the winners need advice. Carla Zilka's new book, *Business Restructuring: An Action Template for Reducing Cost and Growing Profit* provides me with that advice.

I have had the pleasure of knowing Carla Zilka, both personally and professionally, and have come to value her business acumen as well as respect her as an individual. Frankly, when you manage a business, you are responsible not just for the company's performance but also for people's lives, and your decisions have consequences. Making the right decisions during a volatile economy can benefit individuals and their families, while ill-conceived choices can have devastating effects for employees, their families, and their communities. Although Carla is a restructuring expert, I have also found a person that is more than just a cold-hearted consultant; she is someone who cares not only about the bottom line but also about people. This has come through loud and clear in conversations we have had about my business and also as she deals with the same realities of the financial and economic crisis and its impact on her own business, NexGen Advisors,

In *Business Restructuring*, Carla Zilka provides us with her insight from years as one of the most sought-after restructuring advisors to corporate America. She enables the small to midsize company to make educated decisions using methodologies she developed at Fortune 500 companies with which she has worked as an employee and an advisor. Like a good recipe that may be refined and tweaked to suit the tastes of the chef, Carla provides chief executives and their management teams with the "recipe" and the Playbook to execute, then teaches and trains an organization so they can adjust to an ever-changing industry within an ever-changing economic and political environment.

This book is essentially a do-it-yourself guide to restructuring. It should be required reading for CEOs, senior management, and even their employees as they try to "retool" in these challenging times.

William K. Bischoff
Chairman/CEO
FTN Equity Capital Markets

Preface

I began my journey of writing this book almost six months before the macroeconomic climate deteriorated and the financial crisis began. For me, this book represented a new way for companies to view operational restructuring as a means to reduce cost, increase profit, and gain a competitive advantage. By the time the book was half done, the market was declining dramatically every day, and companies' fourth-quarter revenues and earnings were plummeting. Who knew a year ago the market would collapse and we would enter a recession that has instilled fear into the world? As the fear of failure becomes more prevalent in CEOs, Boards of Directors, and senior leaders, the result can be a paralyzing effect, or, worse, action that is short-term tactics performed to meet quarterly numbers. For some, inaction seems safer than taking action, in the hope that they can "wait it out," conducting business as usual. Others conduct hack jobs and cost slashing without a well thought out, long-term strategy.

In my mind, this is absurd. Those who understand the importance of taking action now and commit to a long-term restructuring program recognize that the sooner they get started, the sooner they will reap the benefits and, it is hoped, prevail when others do not. The idea of doing nothing, or sitting on the fence and not deciding whether to move forward or not, instills uncertainty in the organization you are leading. This uncertainty will hurt productivity and the engagement of the employees who are so valuable to making your company successful. Eventually, indecision will lead to stagnant numbers and cause you to fall behind your competitors.

This book is for those who possess the desire and confidence to perform restructuring the "right" way. It is the enabler to help leaders go from good to great, with the goal to change the business model, processes, and organization, to achieve their long-term strategy in the most efficient and effective way possible. It is not intended to be a quick fix or shortcut to reducing cost and growing profit; rather, it is a methodology, approach, and mind-set that should and can be embedded in your organization for long-term sustainable benefits.

In the next nine chapters, you will learn about what restructuring means to me and how my firm and I execute a restructuring program. The text will offer you a framework, process, visuals, and case studies to aid in comprehending what is a complex process. Additionally, I have provided "Quick Tips," which describe things that may not be so visible but will help to facilitate a successful project.

My philosophy on business restructuring rests on the belief that it is a good thing . . . not the negative connotation it has become today. Even the best companies in the world need to assess their organization and processes on a regular basis to ensure their strategic goals can be met. In an effort to drive profit margins up, increase cash flow, and free up monies for capital investments, companies should actively analyze how they can become more productive and efficient to lower their cost structure.

Making your processes as streamlined and automated as possible, and building the right organization structure to execute those processes is crucial in today's economy. You can have the best strategy in the world, but if you do not have the processes and people optimized to execute it, your results may not reach the financial goals you set for the company. And isn't that the name of the game?

Acknowledgments

This book is something that I always dreamed of doing but never thought I would have the time for. But with an ever-changing economy, I figured this was the best time to write about a subject that can actually help the corporate world. When I set out to write a book about something I am passionate about, business restructuring, I thought it would be simple to put into words a methodology and process I have been developing over the past several years. I was wrong!

Although this may not be deemed a technical book, the framework, approach, and tools are very technical in nature, and readers must be acutely aware of how to use them to gain their benefits. Breaking down the processes and providing a step-by-step blueprint to enable readers to implement the framework took input from several people.

First and foremost, I have to thank my Business Process Improvement Practice Leader and Senior Advisor, Paula Zilka Colbert. She also happens to be my twin sister, and I didn't realize how easy it would be for us to collaborate. Our tone and writing styles are exactly the same, and her contribution of all of Chapter 4 and the entire BPI piece was more than I ever asked her to do. Being the overachiever she is, she exceeded my expectations, which is not an easy thing to do. Because she knows the processes as well as I do, she was integral in the review and editing process, looking at every single chapter and visual and providing feedback and comments. I could not have completed this book in the short time frame we had without her help.

Members of my team were also a big part of helping me stay focused on writing. Lena Yim and John Alvino, in true Guardian form, spent months managing the process, with a rigorous project plan, daily meetings, and lots of late nights. Dirk Jonker stepped up and managed the client projects and my firm's operations better than anyone I have ever known, with an energy and passion that clients can't get enough of. Like me, he is compulsively neurotic about getting things done quickly and efficiently, and he managed the firm exquisitely. Hats off to you guys for enabling this book to become a reality for me.

I would also like to thank the contributions from Edward Kim, Managing Director of Synergy Leaders, LLC, and Kaushik Bhaumik, VP & Global Practice Leader, Business Process Outsourcing, Cognizant Technology Solutions. Both Edward and Kaushik share my passion for making companies better and truly understand the importance of business restructuring to achieve this goal.

I would like to thank William (Billy) Bischoff, for writing the foreword that outlined the purpose of the book, and set the tone.

And my dad for his contribution to naming the book . . . who knew a nuclear scientist and engineer could be so creative!

Finally, I would like to thank my editor, Sheck Cho, for making this an absolutely pleasurable experience. I can't wait to write another book for you!

Chapter 1

Restructuring for Success: The 10-Minute Check

Why You Need to Restructure

What exactly is business restructuring? In most cases, the term refers to a turnaround tactic used by distressed companies in an attempt to correct a declining financial situation or climb out of bankruptcy. But business restructuring carries a variety of meanings in business. For a private equity (PE) company, it may mean "financial" restructuring, cleaning and reorganizing the financial books using certain methods of financing, loans, or debt structures. For a chief executive officer (CEO), it may mean cutting heads through reductions in force (RIF) to decrease selling, general, and administrative (SG&A) expense dollars. To me, and for NexGen, it represents a way to build a competitive advantage, which is a good thing, very different from the negative connotations associated with the phrase today.

NexGen is my advisory firm, and we operate by partnering with companies to deliver a vision, strategy, and "playbook" on how to effectively restructure an organization, take costs and waste out of its processes, and design a robust business model. Our patent pending framework drives companies to focus investments and resources on the business core activities, facilitating the reallocation of funds toward growth initiatives, resulting in an increase in revenue and profit margins.

When done correctly, business restructuring is transformational; it offers a way to right-size the company, improve business processes, allocate the right resources against the right activities, and create substantial self-investments geared toward future growth. The scope of this book focuses on "operational" restructuring, a way to fundamentally change your cost structure to deliver the highest value at the lowest cost to your customer. To achieve this, you will need to take a holistic approach and execute a rigid playbook; otherwise, you will not see optimal results. If this is something you cannot commit to for the long haul, do not bother getting started. It is a journey that can take years. It is not for the CEO who wants an instant fix, nor is it for the one managing the business quarter to quarter. There are quick wins when you restructure, but the most impactful changes happen in cycles, and that takes time. Fortunately, if you are dedicated to reading this book, you are already off to a good start.

How do you know if you need to undertake the long journey of restructuring? Well, there is no easy way to determine when you need to restructure, but general guidelines, based on events that may occur within your company, can help you answer that question. Every company, regardless of size or product offering, should take a hard look at itself every year using a rigorous self-assessment to determine what is working in its organization as well as what is not. It is also essential to understand the external environment and how that impacts your business today as well as in the future. Too often we are backward looking and fail to anticipate and properly prepare for crises before they occur. A proactive approach is critical when assessing external market conditions, competitors, and the state of your company.

Exhibit 1.1 demonstrates what I have found to be the natural continuum of a company's thought process when it believes it needs to make improvements. Being cognizant of this cycle and knowing where you fit will help guide you to achieving sustained results.

Usually when my team and I go into a company that thinks it wants to do restructuring, we can already feel the sense of chaos in the environment. The CEO or PE firm has contacted us because the company needs help. Yet, at the topmost level, we get the sense from the leadership team that things are under control. At least that is what most of the leaders are saying. Why would the CEO say things need to be improved but members of the leadership team

Unconscious Incompetence	Conscious Incompetence	Conscious Competence	Unconscious Competence
"We don't know what we don't know."	*"We need to get help in these areas."*	*"We have lots of opportunities to get better."*	*"We have a continuous improvement mind-set."*
Chaos	**Understand**	**Improve**	**Sustain**
• External expertise • Business assessment • Focus on aligning strategic and operational goals • Identify high-risk areas • Assess leadership and skills	• Partner with external experts • CC and II WO!s • OE and PPR WO!s • BPI/BPO road map • Targeted training for skills gaps • Leadership team dynamics optimization		• Continuous improvement culture • BPM implemented • Metrics, KPIs, and SLA actively managed • Knowledge database developed • Knowledge transfer from external experts

Exhibit 1.1   Conscious/Unconscious Chart

claim things are not that bad? Because their decisions and actions caused the problems in the first place! It is a direct reflection on them as leaders. This is even more prevalent in companies with long-tenured executives who grew up in the company. We call this "Unconscious Incompetence," and it is the worst place your company could be on the continuum.

Slightly better, though not ideal, is the company that knows it needs help but also thinks it has the answers to most of the problems. Not really knowing what the root cause issues are, and therefore not being competent to make the correct systemic changes, is a drain on company resources and finances. The worst thing you can do is make assumptions about what you believe the issues are. I call it "intuitive analysis." We had a client who told us the "superstar" finance person knew what was wrong and "where all the dead bodies were." We discovered that she had assumed a lot of the issues, and the company had never done a thorough analysis using data to validate her recommendations. In the end, she was right about the surface issues but not about the root causes. If you do not fix the root cause and only fix the symptoms, you will enter a never-ending cycle of fixing the same issue over and over. If you have not identified the issues using facts, data, and analysis, you do not truly understand the root causes and therefore you are not ready to move down the continuum. This is what we call "Conscious Incompetence."

The next phase of the continuum is "Conscious Competence." Here you have conducted an assessment and understand the source of your issues, as quantified with data-driven evidence. During the assessment, as you peel back the onion and delve deeper into the organization, the opportunities and issues start to surface. Now that you understand the issues, you are conscious of them, but inept when it comes to implementing the changes. You need external resources to help you execute, as with all the continuum's phases.

The final stage of the process is "Unconscious Competence." When you move into action and are conscious of the changes required and have built a competency to make the improvements, you will be able to deliver results by lowering costs and growing profit. Continuous improvement becomes part of the way you run your business. You know how to identify root cause issues and you have embedded the improvement mind-set into the culture through training. You are efficient and effective and able to flex your cost structure. It is a way to gain an advantage over your competitors, prevail in a market downturn, or turn around your company when it is in decline.

Quick Tip

☞ A quick 45- to 60-day assessment by external experts will help you focus on the right issues to attack and is well worth the money.

Are Your Key Financial Indicators Telling You Something?

Getting ahead of your competitors and gaining a competitive advantage is a key reason to perform restructuring. The ability to change cost structure and pricing strategies is an important driver of success in the competitive marketplace. When lower prices are necessary to gain market share, a flexible cost system allows you to change direction without negatively impacting operating margin. Having lower costs and superior service, being able to increase prices in a robust economy or lower prices in a market downturn, are paramount to increasing or maintaining operating margin. Both contribute to increased cash flows, freeing up funds for operating expenses, capital investments, and/or acquisitions.

If you struggle either to increase or to maintain operating margin, some key indicators related to your cost structure will point to common issues immediately. The two important financial indicators in Exhibit 1.2 outline some of the metrics you should be looking at carefully on a regular basis. The exhibit presents a couple of

Metric	Best in Class
Revenue growth	9% improvement
Profitability	9% improvement

Exhibit 1.2 Year–Over–Year Financial Indicators
SOURCE: Aberdeen Group—October 17, 2007
A benchmark study by Aberdeen Group, a Harte-Hanks company, co-sponsored by Dundas, iDashboards, Insightformation, Corda, and Actuate.

best-in-class benchmarks that you can use to compare against your own performance. How well do you match up against benchmark?

Other indicators including cash flow, SG&A as a percentage of revenue, full-time equivalents (FTEs) as a percentage of revenue, and specific departmental budgets as a percentage of revenue (such as research and development [R&D] or marketing) will also give you an indication of how well you are doing against benchmark, if you can trend them monthly, quarterly, and annually. David Hatch, Research Director of the Business Intelligence practice at the Aberdeen Group, a premier research and analysis firm, said this about measuring key indicators:

> Businesses thrive or fail based on their ability to identify, define, track and act upon key performance metrics/indicators (KPIs). Executives and line-of-business management are increasingly feeling the pressure to establish the right KPIs to enable timelier and more accurate decisions. The faster and more accurately KPIs can be accessed, reviewed, analyzed and acted upon, the better chance an organization has for success.[1]

When assessing the financial "health" of a company, visible symptoms may or may not be obvious. The obvious financial symptoms included a negative or declining cash flow and reduction in operating margin percentage. Another very telling financial indicator is SG&A. When evaluating SG&A as a percentage of revenue and comparing it against the total number of employees, typically, the smaller the percentage SG&A is of revenue, the better. Most industries should focus on assessing opportunities to eliminate cost from

SG&A line items. By comparing an individual company to the industry and broader sector, a company can quickly determine if SG&A expense is within reason. The average SG&A as a percentage of revenue for a best-in-class company is between 9 and 12 percent. The average among Fortune 100 companies, however, is between 14 and 16 percent.[2] Now, drill down to a lower level, and consider the consumer goods sector as an example. Its SG&A average runs in the 19 percent range. For the apparel industry, within the consumer goods sector, the average SG&A as a percentage of revenue is 39 percent.[3] The SG&A is considerably higher than best-in-class, Fortune 100, and the consumer goods sector average, while the number of employees is much lower. Each individual company must determine for itself whether the high cost of SG&A is justified. In the apparel industry, much funding is invested in marketing and advertising, as retailers sell new styles at least four times per year. Another reason for the high SG&A for the apparel industry is that most retailers source their goods internationally from local suppliers, which results in high shipping costs, import fees, and considerable logistics management. But even within the apparel industry, some companies have much higher SG&A costs than their competitors.

Why is this? Take a look at Exhibit 1.3. Is it just advertising, or is overhead and structure not optimal? Are there middleman activities that can be eliminated with newly reengineered, robust processes and systems? Can noncore transactional activities be outsourced? This assessment presents the opportunity to take cost out by redesigning the organization structure and reengineering or outsourcing the supporting processes.

The more interesting financial symptoms are those that are not so obvious. In each of NexGen's client companies, little or no technology investments were made toward standardized platforms to maximize efficiency. The existing systems were disparate, standalone, self-built platforms that were difficult to integrate. This siloed application resulted in inefficient organizations coupled with disconnected, process-driven systems. Lack of technology investment

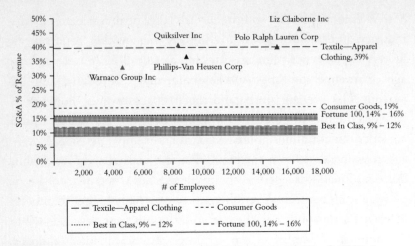

Exhibit 1.3 Year-Over-Year Financial Indicators with Graph (SG&A versus Employees)

SOURCE: SG&A and employee information from finance.google.com year-end 2008.

inhibits the ability of a business to optimize processes and people. In my experience, information technology (IT) capital has a greater impact on work productivity than non-IT related investments. Leading companies use robust technology to support business processes and have the ability to maintain consistent real-time information. They also streamline processes with business partners and customers and make information available on a global scale. Often companies need to make investment or operational decisions but do not have the most comprehensive data. Technology, paired with optimized processes, enables the power of agility and is critical for any company to maintain a competitive edge.

Many of the basic financial indicators that companies track are just not enough to determine how well they are doing. In some cases, these indicators can give the leadership team the wrong message regarding the health of their business. Measuring metrics through detailed dashboards and scorecards of work activities that roll up to your main business processes is required in order to understand the overall health of the company.

While the SG&A graph displays the financial health of an organization, you can ask yourself some basic questions to determine how the heart of the organization's operations is performing. The financials are backward looking, and as discussed, that is not the best way to understand the future. However, your operations can help you predict challenges and issues that will not show up in the financials for at least a quarter or more.

If we break down the "heart" of the organization into operations, organization, and process, we can ask the right questions and look at the right data to make a quick diagnosis: Are we healthy or not? It is this 10-Minute Check that will tell you how "Conscious" or "Unconscious" you are and the level of restructuring that is required.

I can tell where the company stands on the "Conscious/ Unconscious" Continuum just by asking the leadership team a couple of standard questions. In some cases, the leaders cannot answer the questions, and that is the first sign of chaos deeper in the organization. It is dangerous when you think about it. The bottom line is that "strategy is executed from the ranks,"[4] and it is important to ask the questions to the people in the mid to lower levels of the organization. They know what is going on and will be able to tell you what needs to be fixed.

Quick Tip

☞ Conduct "skip-level" meetings with high-potential employees every year. These meetings should be with employees one level below your direct reports. The leadership team should get in this habit as well. The information you gain will be invaluable. These meetings are great ways to understand the true issues hindering your organization.

As a matter of fact, most operations people know how "immature" or "mature" their processes are and how effectively they can deliver to the customer. They have a good idea of what the customer wants and what new products, offerings, and markets are important to invest in.

They also know what needs to happen to deliver on the strategy yet very often they are not involved in the delivery process. Most strategies are built from the top down, with limited visibility into the day-to-day challenges that stop the company from delivering the highest value to the customer. How can a company's leadership stay on top of issues and redirect strategies if required? Set up a Strategy Council.

Quick Tip

☞ Form a *Strategy Council* that includes lower-level operations people and build a strategic architecture that represents what you can truly deliver today and over the next three years. Include this group in merger and acquisition discussions and strategy reviews to get a clear picture of where to invest for organic and inorganic growth opportunities and to help mitigate any roadblocks that may stop you from achieving your short- and long-term strategy.

Go through the 10-Minute Checklist in Exhibit 1.4 and see how you score. You or someone on your team should be able to answer these questions quickly. If it takes days, that is a bad sign.

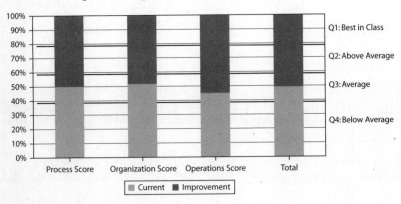

Exhibit 1.4 10-Minute Checklist
SOURCE: Aberdeen Group—Mon Apr 14, 2008
Live Analysis of Operations Management Benchmark Data Reveals Best-In-Class Manufacturing Strategies.
Aberdeen's benchmark Manufacturing Operations Management Study Senior Analyst Matthew Littlefield.

10

Restructuring for Success: The 10-Minute Check

Process	Score	Rating
How many of your processes are standardized across the company?		
How many of your processes are automated using a technology platform or tools?		
Which processes do you continually improve to deliver better performance?		
How many of your processes are measured?		All = 5
How many of your processes are measured against benchmark?		Most = 4 Some = 3
How many of your processes are outsourced?		Few = 2
How many of your processes have process owners?		None = 1
How many of your processes have KPIs that are linked to corporate strategy AND operational goals?		
Do you measure the "relationship" with your "customer"?		
Does your customer ever see "defects" out of your process?		
Process Total Score		
Organization	Score	Rating
Do you conduct a company-wide organization analysis of spans of control and number of layers?		
How many of your functions conduct an organization analysis of spans of control annually?		All = 5 Most = 4 Some = 3
How many of your functions benchmark the number of FTEs annually?		Few = 2
Do you know the average span of control for managers in your company?		None = 1
Do you have centers of excellence for areas of expertise?		Yes = 5
Do you have shared services for administrative and transactional activities?		No = 3
Do you have a pay-for-performance compensation plans?		Don't know = 0
Do you have an organization that focuses on continuous improvement?		
Do you have a training program for Six Sigma or continuous improvement?		
Organization Total Score		
Operations	Score	Rating
Is your supply chain integrated as one process and organization?		
Do your policies and procedures get in the way of quick decision making and taking action?		Yes = 5
Do you have too many reports?		No = 3 Don't know = 0
Is data readily available?		
Operations Total Score		
Grand Total Score		

Exhibit 1.4   (*Continued*)

11

Was any of the material presented thus far surprising to you? A "yes" answer is a good indicator that you need to take action. Chapter 2 lays out exactly what you need to do.

Notes

1. Operational KPIs and Performance Management by David Hatch, Aberdeen Group, August 2008
2. Deloitte Value Analytics, 2006. Copyright © 2006 Deloitte Development LLC. All rights reserved.
3. Tim Lau, NexGen Advisors Study, 2009.
4. HBR, "Building an Organized Process for Strategy Communication," *Balanced Scorecard Report 9*, No. 3 (May–June 2007).

Chapter 2

The Playbook: A Comprehensive Approach

Creating a Foundation for Success

As you read in Chapter 1, business restructuring is an effective way to lower costs. The current economic climate has prompted more and more companies to look for savings opportunities that drive margin improvement and ultimately realize earnings growth. To get there, though, your company needs a restructuring playbook, something to guide your execution of this comprehensive approach. It starts with a model, an integrated plan with multiple workstreams and infrastructural elements that allows you to leverage several efficiency methods simultaneously. Exhibit 2.1 is the framework I developed at NexGen Advisors and have implemented for several Fortune 1000 companies.

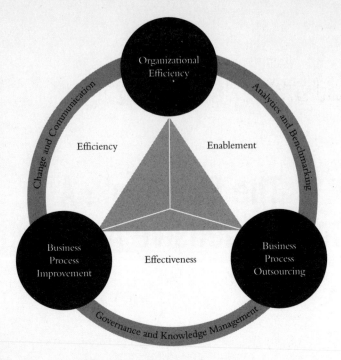

Exhibit 2.1 NexGen's Holistic Framework
©2009

The framework infrastructure is key to building the program on solid ground. As in construction, a strong foundation is essential to building a durable, stable structure. The same concepts apply when developing a business restructuring program. Skimp here, and you will have limited your chances of a successful outcome.

FRAMEWORK FOUNDATIONAL ELEMENTS:

1. Analytics and Benchmarking
2. Change Management and Communication
3. Governance and Knowledge Management

At the core of the model are data, analytics, and benchmarking. Most companies have plenty of data, but few use it in a way that helps drive the business to make informed decisions. The data model will determine how accurately you can forecast and manage business performance. It is also the critical input into tools and processes to identify opportunities for improvement.

Having clean data in a form that adds value and is useful to a business is a basic requirement that most CEOs and senior leaders overlook. They think it is the job of the Chief Information Officer (CIO) to build the data model that deliver the reports and analytics they need. In actuality, it is the CEO's responsibility as the "customer" of the data outputs to define what the data should tell them. Most times when we go into a company and begin to analyze the maturity of their data model, we get blank stares. They say, "What do you mean? We have a lot of data and track many metrics." Our response, "You have a lot of data, but it doesn't deliver the *right* reports and metrics." Too much data causes analysis paralysis and requires many resources to decipher what it is saying. A few key reports and metrics are all that is required to understand the status of the company, and typically speaking, less is more.

Not sure if your data model is operating properly? Here is a quick test. Ask your Chief Financial Officer (CFO), Senior Vice President (SVP) of human resources, and SVP of sales to provide you with one standard report each:

- Human Resources: Weekly headcount report
- Sales: Weekly sales figures report
- Finance: Weekly cash flow report

If the company's systems are integrated and run on an enterprise system, and if it takes them more than 24 hours to deliver these three reports, you have a problem. The data model was not set up properly, or the system may be cumbersome to use, so people have developed Excel spreadsheets as the chosen "tool" to manage reports and data, causing time delays.

I will never forget the response I received when I was facilitating a finance Work-Out with a technology company that makes products for the financial services industry. I asked what data model they were using for basic reporting and how efficient their monthly close process was. The overwhelming response was that they did everything on Excel spreadsheets! They pulled the data from the system but then imported it into Excel so they could manipulate it to show what the leadership team wanted to see. This was shocking, considering that the company had implemented Oracle Financials throughout most of its global enterprise over the last two years. Their mistake? Shortcuts. The lack of standardized reports, which would have enabled everyone to be "automated," along with the lack of training on the functionality of the system, led to gross inefficiencies, much of which the CFO was not even aware. The resources required simply to roll up the numbers every month far exceeded what would have been required had the company taken the time to set up the standard reports and train a few people on how to pull them automatically.

If systems are not integrated and are a mix of legacy and homegrown, then you have another problem. This situation occurs when little or no investment is made to financial systems to make data flow seamlessly. Take a good look at your capital expenditures and reallocate money to fix this . . . immediately! This is a high priority.

> **Quick Tip**
>
> ☞ Hire a Data Modeler and get the systems delivering the reports you need to see with a click of the mouse. If the systems are not integrated, put money aside and invest in integrating the systems. It is vital that the systems are able to talk to each other and pull the data required to deliver automated reports rather than using Excel spreadsheets, where errors can, and do, frequently occur.

If data is one of the key foundational elements, then analytics and benchmarking are the outputs that tell the story of the health of an organization. This is vital information that should be checked quarterly or, at a minimum, annually and should become part of the business's operating rhythm. A full benchmarking study on processes and organization efficiency should be implemented at a minimum every two years. Once you have the baseline, you can use the metrics as part of your goals, objectives, and key performance indicators (KPIs) for performance management.

There are three ways to benchmark:

1. Purchase standard benchmarks.
2. Engage in a customized study.
3. Create internal benchmarks.

The first and most common option is to purchase benchmarks already calculated by industry in the form of a metrics database through an external source, such as the American Productivity & Quality Center (APQC) or Hackett. However, in order for these benchmarks to be effective, in-house experts must know how to use them.

You can also purchase a more detailed customized benchmarking study from external sources, but this requires input from the company on specific metrics it is trying to measure and peer group participation in the survey. Although it is the most accurate form of benchmarking, it also takes the most time, and peers may decide not to participate. Again, make sure you have identified the right metrics and have the internal competency to use benchmarks.

The final option is an internal assessment across your enterprise, by region and function, to determine best practices within your organization and to create the baseline that other groups will be measured against. This method takes the least amount of time and requires the least amount of investment, but it does not give you a clear line of sight into how you match up against your competitors or peer group.

There are advantages to all of these methods, but you should view benchmarks as a guide and a goal. Every company has its own idiosyncrasies, which make it difficult to have true apples-to-apples comparisons across an industry. Pick the right approach for you, but at least look to an external source to get an idea of where you stand within your industry. Creating this baseline is fundamental to reducing cost and driving toward best in class. A word of caution: Do not let the organization use the excuse that the benchmarks are not viable because your business model is so "different." This is never the case. Every business is different, but there are common processes and activities that all businesses execute, regardless of the product or service. Using this excuse is often a clear indication of resistance to change.

Another building block to your foundation is a change management and communications (CMC) strategic plan. A CMC strategic plan sets the tone and creates the new culture that will be needed to sustain the changes you are about make. As you know, any change, even a positive one, is difficult for employees to accept. And if employees do not support the changes, nothing will get accomplished. They are the ones to execute the changes and continue to sustain them after the transformation is complete. If there is one thing that will sink your restructuring effort, it is a resistant corporate culture. Corporate culture is inherent in every company, and it can have a positive or negative influence on your restructuring effort. It is paramount to understand your culture so that an effective CMC plan can be developed. If everyone is not aligned, collaboration will be impossible.

The goal is to create a vision the employees can relate to—almost a new identity—which will motivate them to move forward. The CMC plan should convey what work life will be like in the new transformed company, satisfying the age-old question, "What's in it for me?"

CEOs and leaders have a choice when launching a restructuring initiative. You can choose to be *closed* about the process and communicate only when major milestones have been met, or you can be *open* and communicate frequently and directly about the methods, the results, and the expectations, including potential job losses. My view is always to be open and honest. And it cannot just come from the top. In most restructuring programs, CEOs tend to be the ones driving the communication downward. The senior leaders in the organization have to be just as knowledgeable about the processes and status in order to truly effect change. They are important change agents and must come with an open mind about the current state and not be in denial or against any change, as we have seen in many companies. Getting the message out to employees is crucial, and building a CMC plan at every level of the company is the only way to achieve this.

One of the key activities you can do to ensure the employees are getting the messages the senior leaders deliver is to adopt an employee perspective through a Pulse Survey. This is not an engagement survey but a very focused tool that will keep your finger on the pulse of how the organization feels about the restructuring activities. This is important because most employees are not as involved as senior leadership, and therefore are not as confident in the improvements and changes about to occur. The Pulse Survey will give you a week-by-week or month-by-month view of how the organization feels at that moment and will speak volumes to you.

The third foundational piece is governance and knowledge management. Putting the right team together to execute the model and drive the transition and changes will be critical to maintaining the progression forward to the "new identity." Program governance will be the way to track the progress and make decisions.

The first decision is the CEO's: Who does he or she put in charge of the initiative as the Sponsor and Champion? If you did not answer "ME!" then you have failed Restructuring 101. The biggest mistake a CEO can make is not to be intimately involved in the restructuring details and make it a priority. After all, the CEO is running the company. Restructuring is as important and delivers the same financial and operational benefits as any other item on the CEO's plate. When a CEO puts someone else in charge as the Sponsor or Champion, the employees know he or she is not engaged, and they begin to question the validity of the program.

In one company we worked with, the CEO delegated to his CFO, and immediately the Pulse Survey showed red across the board, but especially on questions about trusting the senior management on the initiative. Delegating is a nonsensical excuse for not wanting to deal with the details and issues that will most likely come from such an initiative. It indicates to everyone involved a lack of leadership. Even if you cannot stomach the details and issues and want to delegate, do not put the CFO in charge. CFOs typically are financially focused individuals who may have a difficult time understanding the long-term approach and investments required to make a restructuring program work. They are focused on looking at the numbers quarter to quarter and may not make the right decisions to benefit the company in the long run. Let them count the money, and leave transforming the company to someone who has a visionary mind-set.

> **Quick Tip**
>
> ☞ Put the Chief Operating Officer, Chief Information Officer, or strategy head in charge of managing the project day to day as the Restructuring Lead. They have the vision to understand the future state and will be more open-minded about the journey ahead.

So now that we know who will be the Sponsor, Champion, and the Restructuring Lead, we need a body that will be responsible

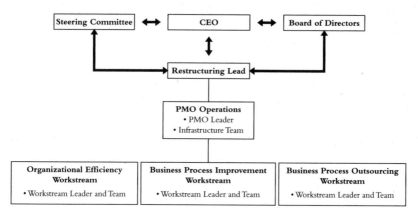

Exhibit 2.2   Governance Chart

for decision making: the Steering Committee. As you can see from Exhibit 2.2, you will need a strong representation of cross-functional experts who understand the issues and challenges the business is facing.

They will be responsible for making decisions and approving reductions and investments, and are accountable for the performance of the restructuring plan. They are also the owners of the timeline and should be able to answer these questions:

- Where are we? = Current state
- How far do we need to go? = Future state

You should have at least 6 to 10 people on the Steering Committee, each representing a different function and/or region of the company. One company we worked with had only three people on the committee, because one was always missing, it was difficult to get decisions made quickly. Make sure to choose progressive, outside-the-box thinkers as well as those who tend to question and ask for details. Find people who have come from outside the company to get an external point of view.

While the Steering Committee is governing the initiative, the PMO is enabling the transition to occur.

Transition management includes two areas: knowledge management and training. This team will be responsible for the knowledge management database that will house all the documents, processes, and tool kits the organization develops during the program and will be using moving forward. There are many types of shared web-based products, or you may have a shared drive you use internally. Either is fine, just make sure it is accessible to everyone in the company and has search capability built into it so it is easy and efficient to use.

One of the most comprehensive knowledge management systems I have ever seen was when I was at GE. To this day, I am still in awe of the system's capability. You could go to the search engine and type anything into it, and within seconds, Subject Matter Expert (SME) names and contact information, best practices, templates, case studies, and examples would appear. You could ask questions to the SMEs and get help with virtually any issue you were dealing with. It had over 1 million hits a month . . . truly innovative at the time.

What if you do not have a knowledge management database? Build one ASAP! You do not need anything as complicated as GE's, just a simply repository. Get your CIO on this quickly and have it ready in time to start loading information from the program team and experts.

Training employees on the new processes, tool kits, and systems is an area most companies overlook, but that is impractical. People cannot be expected to change the way they have always done something unless someone teaches them otherwise. Imagine spending time, money, and resources to create new and improved processes, develop better technology and tool kits, but not institute a robust training effort to teach the organization how to use them.

Most companies have training in the human resources (HR) function, but this training is different from traditional competency training. The knowledge management group will manage the transition to the "new identity" and train employees on how to utilize the new and improved processes, tools, and technology. It should be a team comprised of SMEs in Six Sigma and Lean, experts in the technology platforms the company uses, and change management and communication experts

If the changes are not implemented quickly and the people are not trained properly, they will just revert back to the old way of doing things, and all with be for naught.

Quick Tip

☞ Set a budget for a knowledge management database and a training plan, and identify an owner who will make it happen.

Flexible Platform for Achieving Results

Now that you have all the foundational pieces in place—data analytics and benchmarking, change management and communications, governance and transition management—it is time to move onto the integrated workstreams. Each workstream can be executed separately, but the results will not be optimal. The best results come when you use the road map in Exhibit 2.3 to execute short-, mid-, and long-term improvements.

On average, a restructuring plan using this framework takes approximately 24 to 36 months from inception to "control" phase, meaning the improvements are complete and the company is realizing the financial opportunities identified in the assessment. By this time you should be managing the results using the standard benchmarks and metrics defined in the beginning of the program and have set up a Continuous Improvement organization whose responsibility is to incrementally improve the processes and drive toward operational excellence.

Activities	Year 1				Year 2				Year 3			
	Q1	Q2	Q3	Q4	Q1	Q2	Q3	Q4	Q1	Q2	Q3	Q4
45–60 Day Assessment												
Organizational Efficiency Workstream												
Analytics and Diagnostic												
Leadership Team Dynamics												
Workouts!												
Iterative Organizational Design Workouts												
Business Process Improvement Workstream												
Assessment												
Define/Measure/Project Identification												
Improve/Control												
Metric Scorecard												
Business Process Outsourcing Workstream												
Scope Opportunities/Sourcing Strategy												
Go to Market RFPs												
Negotiate Contracts												
Transiton to Suppliers												
Scorecard Performance												
Infrastructure												
Data and Benchmarking												
Change Management and Communications												
Governance and Knowledge Management (Training)												
Business Process Management Dashboard												

Exhibit 2.3 Restructuring Timeline

The framework consists of three separate and distinct work-steams whose interdependencies form the recipe that drives the program to optimal results and build a competitive, flexible cost structure. Executing one workstream will deliver results, but not to the level an integrated approach does.

Although the worksteams have different activities, they are depend on each other, with the outputs of one being the inputs into another. This constant flow of data and information becomes a fluid approach to changing your company's business model.

The three workstreams are:

1. Organization Efficiency (OE)
2. Business Process Improvement (BPI)
3. Business Process Outsourcing (BPO)

We start with OE, which is the most iterative of the three workstreams. It delivers short- and midterm improvements and cost savings, and focuses on the structure of the organization. It aims to increase the efficiency and effectiveness of your structure and the productivity of your employees.

The first step is to "right-size" the organization by conducting an organizational diagnostic analysis, including span of control (number of direct reports managed by a manager) and layers. In most cases, companies are grossly outside of the benchmarks when it comes to spans of leadership and number of layers in the organization. The initial cost reductions will come from increasing spans and de-layering, typically in the management layers.

There are several processes and tools to gain organizational efficiency, but the way most companies do it is by conducting a reduction in force (RIF), which can be random in nature and leave the company with inadequate resources to perform business activities. In almost every assessment we have conducted for clients, they will tell us they have performed RIFs and that they are lean. Yet our analysis shows that they are over benchmark in number of layers and spans of leadership. The goal is to understand the benchmarks and to continually drive the organization structure to meet them. Each function and business unit has its own set of benchmarks, which should be tracked annually.

The OE workstream is a critical input into the mid- and long-term improvement workstreams, BPI and BPO. The right-sizing of the organization is only the first step in OE. The continued tweaking of the organization structure occurs when the BPI and BPO workstreams have executed their improvements: streamlining, reengineering, and outsourcing processes. As the processes become more efficient and automated, they require fewer people to execute them. As a result, redesigning the organization again with additional reductions in headcount will be required. As part of the continuous improvement approach and mind-set, your company should realign and reallocate human capital frequently

The BPI workstream consists of several areas of expertise using Six Sigma as the basis for improving the processes. Types of Six Sigma methodologies that are utilized include Lean Sigma, Theory of Constraints (TOC), and At the Customer, For the Customer (ACFC).

The main goal of BPI is to reduce redundancies and process inefficiencies in order to become more customer-focused and market driven. This approach addresses legacy process inefficiencies by focusing on identifying waste in the processes and systems and on creating a streamlined, accurate execution of business process across multiple business units, locations, and functional areas. Standardization is the key to reducing variation, which in turn reduces defects and eliminates rework and waste.

The BPO workstream focuses on what processes have limited strategic value to the business but are mature in the outsourcing market and, therefore, would be good candidates for a shared service, offshoring, or business process outsourcing. A sourcing strategy must be designed first, by conducting an internal cost and productivity analysis against current market pricing through domestic and

Success Factors	Derailers
Engaged leadership who are change leaders and develop communication plans to share updates and wins throughout their organization	Leaders who give lip service or are detached and don't support changes, exhibited by pulse survey results of lack of communication down in the organization
Dedicated, top talent resources whose only job is to work on the restructuring program	Employees doing two jobs, continuing to keep responsibilities for current job and a role on the restructuring team
Long-term, annual focus with investment dollars built into program and ROI over multiple years	Short-term, quarter-to-quarter focus, focused on immediate cost cutting and limited or no budget for investments
Process owner and senior leadership responsible for results, and compensation linked to metrics	Pushing ownership of results to restructuring team and not giving financial incentives for their success
Open and honest communication to the employees on next steps and activities to occur, including RIFs, celebratiion of wins	Closed, under-the-covers approach, with no line of sight for the employees, RIFs come as a surprise and shock the organization

Exhibit 2.4   Success Factors and Derailers

offshore suppliers. An input to this workstream is the BPI outputs of the Business Core Competency Model, a make versus buy analysis that identifies which business processes are the most viable for the BPO workstream.

The OE workstream is integrated into the BPO process and transition to an external vendor, and the organization is again "sized" based on the activities the retained organization will be performing.

By now, you should have a clear picture of the framework and all the moving parts. Because of the intricacy of the approach, there are important success factors and derailers, listed in Exhibit 2.4, that we have experienced in our many engagements. These problems may seem like common sense, but quite often they are overlooked or seen as trivial. They are not! Missing one can set you behind or off-kilter, and the effort to get it back on track is far more difficult than if you had set them as principles initially. Opting out of any of these is a nonnegotiable.

Now that you have a playbook and understand the framework and approach, it is time to get into the details regarding the resources, processes, and tools you will need to launch and execute the program. Architecting a successful restructuring project takes a significant amount of planning. Chapter 3 will help you put the playbook into action.

Chapter 3

Putting the Playbook into Action

Building a Winning Team

They say that good planning contributes 80 percent to the success of any project, and I could not agree more. Managing the logistics to develop a project that eventually will morph into a new competency and become a way of doing business is not an easy task. The team that you will create is akin to the Special Forces picked to carry out a mission. Choose the members of this team wisely. These people will be responsible for driving the company to performance excellence, which will in turn deliver the savings and revenue opportunities that were identified during the assessment.

In Chapter 2, we talked about the Restructuring Lead's role as well as the role of the Steering Committee. Exhibit 3.1 outlines

29

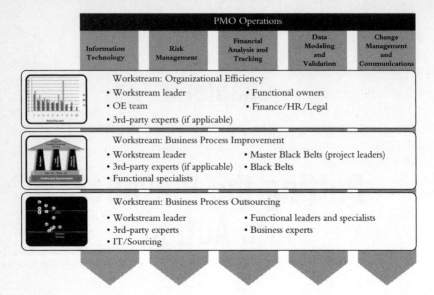

PMO Operations				
Information Technology	Risk Management	Financial Analysis and Tracking	Data Modeling and Validation	Change Management and Communications

Workstream: Organizational Efficiency
- Workstream leader
- OE team
- 3rd-party experts (if applicable)
- Functional owners
- Finance/HR/Legal

Workstream: Business Process Improvement
- Workstream leader
- 3rd-party experts (if applicable)
- Functional specialists
- Master Black Belts (project leaders)
- Black Belts

Workstream: Business Process Outsourcing
- Workstream leader
- 3rd-party experts
- IT/Sourcing
- Functional leaders and specialists
- Business experts

Exhibit 3.1   Project Infrastructure

the rest of the team. Proper governance and execution are critical success factors, so a strong, cohesive team that understands the importance and direction of the project is vital.

Clearly define all roles and responsibilities at the project's inception to ensure there are no overlaps or gaps in the activities about to be executed. We like to use a RASCI model, similar to the one depicted in Exhibit 3.2, to kick off a project and review ownership of all activities and deliverables.

The elements of RASCI[1] are:

R = **Responsible**. Person who owns the problem/project.

A = to whom "R" is **Accountable**. He or she must sign or approve the work before it is okay.

S = can be **Supportive**. Can provide resources or can play a supporting role in implementation.

C = should be **Consulted**. Has information and/or capacity necessary to complete the work.

I = should be **Informed**. Must be notified of results, but need not be consulted.

	Program Manager	PM Assistant	Board of Directors	Service Manager	Legal Advisor
Activity 1	R		A		
Activity 2	A	R		S	C
Activity 3	RA		I		I
Activity 4	RA				C
Activity 5	A	R		S	

Exhibit 3.2   RASCI Model

Only after you have reviewed the roles and responsibilities with the team members, and signed off on them, can you move forward and launch the project. This exercise must engage everyone involved in the project, including external vendors and consultants. It should also be used in the performance management process. The team members' execution of their responsibilities and deliverables are considered their goals and objectives, and should be considered when they are being rated on performance.

Quick Tip

☞ If you do not have access to a RASCI model, just ask your HR department. They either will have one handy or will know where to get one for you quickly.

To build the RASCI model, you must first understand the definitions of the roles and responsibilities for each participant, which are provided below. Use these descriptions of the various roles as a guide when identifying the resources that will make up the team as well as what their primary function will be. We start at the governing body, the Steering Committee.

Steering Committee

The Steering Committee is the decision-making body for your restructuring endeavor. Members of this committee provide guidance on the project and work closely to ensure that it delivers the best possible results for the company as a whole. The individuals who make up this committee are called Champions, and they encourage execution by communicating the project's priority to their colleagues as well as by fostering an overall sense of urgency in the culture. The committee, led by the Restructuring Lead, should immediately establish a standard operating rhythm whereby it meets at least once each week.

Members of the Steering Committee are usually one or two levels down in the organization, open minded, and knowledgeable in a diverse set of disciplines. A good mix typically engages multiple functions: marketing, R&D, operations, HR, IT, legal, and finance. Each one offers a different viewpoint to the decisions that need to be made. In order to keep the culture change consistent and even throughout, it is important to engage all facets of the business right away. If you are a CEO or president and you have a small executive leadership team, you may find it useful to include the entire team on the Steering Committee. This way, you can meld it into your weekly senior management team meetings. An appropriate time allotment for these meetings is one to two hours per week.

Restructuring Lead

The Restructuring Lead oversees the project and manages the communication of its status to the Steering Committee, the CEO, and the board of directors. This person has the most strategic role on the team, acting as the team's main change agent and motivator. Restructuring Leads are great communicators. They emphasize the positive impact this project will deliver and demonstrate its importance with their sense of urgency toward solving issues that arise from it. They are the orchestra's conductors, and they need to be able to lead a team and drive toward the future state.

CFOs often fill this role, but I believe that is a mistake. Earlier, we talked about how transforming a business is a visionary effort, and many finance people will not be able to pull themselves away from their financial tasks to see the forest for the trees. The best leaders are strategy or operations resources. Strategy resources see the future state and can track toward it, while operations people live it every day and can make quick adjustments to the plan to avoid bumps in the road.

PMO Leader

The Project Management Office (PMO) Leader is in charge of running the project day to day and preferably should be trained in Six Sigma. Other PMO Lead responsibilities include connecting daily with the Restructuring Lead, Workstream Leads, communications, and PMO operations.

Quick Tip

☞ If you do not have a Six Sigma Master Black Belt or certified PMI (Project Management Institute) to use, it is recommended that you either hire an expert or seek professional help from a company that specializes in it. The investment is worth every cent when the project is run well, on time, and on budget.

This is probably the most important role on the team. The PMO Leader ensures that the project plan and resources function properly. This person must have strong project management skills, including the ability to orchestrate a large team. Whether your company is big or small, the importance of this role must not be overlooked. We have all heard the phrase "Time is money." As the person managing the timing of the project, the PMO lead is also indirectly controlling how much the project costs. If the lead is good at what he or she does, you will complete projects early, which will increase productivity and realize savings at an accelerated rate from what was originally projected. Look for someone who can offer hands-on support; it is a key attribute for this role.

PMO Operations

PMO operations supports the workstreams, PMO Leader, and Restructuring Lead and provides the infrastructure that will enable the execution of the framework. The members of the PMO operations team come from several disciplines to ensure the project runs on time, on budget, and delivers support to the workstreams, which is required for them to execute their tasks. Your organization may be big enough and have enough talent so that you can have one owner for each discipline, or you may be smaller and not have enough people to own one area. If you need to combine roles, you can, as long as the tasks are completed accurately and efficiently. The choice is yours. In my experience, one owner per area works best.

Information Technology Leader

Information technology manages the implementation of technology changes as a result of workstream outputs and is responsible for setting up and delivering the metrics dashboard and knowledge management system.

IT Leaders are critical for two reasons.

1. They own the prioritization of the data request for the initial 45- to 60-day assessment as well as the data requirements for the workstream during the restructuring project.

34

2. They have to be willing to drive changes within the current systems or even implement new systems based on recommendations that come out of the workstreams.

The IT Leader should be knowledgeable about all the systems in the company and seen as a strategic individual who says, "YES, WE CAN DO IT!" He or she must be open and willing to cooperate as well as innovate when new systems or applications are needed. An IT person who says "We can't get that data" or "It would be too difficult to get that data" or is reluctant to make changes to the current systems (let alone replace them!) is not needed for this project.

It is very important for the IT Leader to work with the Data Modeling and Validation team to ensure that the data is clean and is a sample that represents activities of the company as a whole. The person doesn't need to be the CIO of the company or even a division CIO but should be well respected within the organization. The company's CIO must be supportive of this individual, allowing the IT Leader to make decisions in a timely manner, which usually means with little oversight. Ultimately, this person ends up being the project manager for all the systems changes and new installations related to the restructuring project. This role works collaboratively with the workstream leads to define the technology strategy needed to implement the changes the project indicates are necessary.

Risk Management

The Risk Management Leader is the team member who manages the "risks, mitigants, and interdependencies"—outputs from the workstreams—and ensures business continuity. This person is responsible for contingency plans and sign off on reduction in force practices, severance packages, and any other procedures that may have legal impact.

As the person responsible for ensuring that there is no business interruption and that the improvements do not impact the current business environment negatively, the Risk Management

35

Leader holds a lot of responsibility and are required to question the changes if they feel the business will suffer. It is an auditor type of role. The person in the position will be expected to work with the workstream leads, PMO Leader, and Restructuring Lead to monitor business performance before and after changes are made. The Risk Management Leader must understand business operations and devise a clear information channel to the leadership to gain insight into any issues that may be bubbling up.

Financial Analysis and Tracking

The Financial Analysis and Tracking Lead oversees the financial opportunities identified during the assessment and tracks the progress toward goals set by the Restructuring Lead and Steering Committee. This individual conducts financial analysis for adverse impact, severance, capital investments, revenue recognition, and so on.

Finance Leads track the project's savings, revenue opportunities, and cost/benefit analysis. This position needs someone well versed in financial policies and rules but who is also a great analyst. A Financial Analyst with a CPA is preferred but not required. This person should not be a manager but should have the respect of the team to ensure that requests are received on time. The Finance Lead tracks the project financials, including the dashboard, and juggles many critical tasks that need to be completed at the same time, so a good multitasker is necessary. He or she must interact often with the CEO and leadership team, so it is important to have someone that can clearly articulate the details of the savings/opportunities templates and dashboard. Early in the project, the Steering Committee should agree on the length of time that the project will be tracked. At the very least, it should be for 12 months after all the recommendations are implemented and any outsourcing has been transferred, so a year-over-year comparison can be made. Therefore, the Finance Leader is the last person to leave the team. He or she may have less to do as the project winds down and moves into a smooth operating mode, but continuing to track key metrics is critical to ensuring success.

Data Modeling and Validation

The Data Modeling and Validation team owns the data model and reports required to manage project and business. This group is responsible for delivering on data requests from the workstreams and for validating data based on source information.

The person responsible for the data modeling and validation that occurs up front and throughout the project should be from the IT function, an Internal Auditor (if the role exists) or a Six Sigma Black Belt. Regardless of the function this resource comes from, he or she must have functional and operational knowledge of the system in order to understand how the data is captured and what the outputs will look like. This role is a combined role, with responsibilities changing during the project when the role transitions from Data Validator to Data Modeler.

The main role of the Data Validator is to ensure the data complies with the request, is clean, and is a statistically valid sample size that will allow accurate conclusions to be drawn. If this person does not understand what the output of the data should look like, why there are outliers, or if the data is wrong (i.e., 00/00/00 as a date), the analysis will be wrong and there will be little hope of finding root causes. Therefore, this person is also responsible for auditing and signing off on the data before it is handed over to the teams that eventually will use it for analysis. If the data is not clean, the Data Validator will work with the appropriate IT person to obtain acceptable data for the current request, and change the system or inputs to ensure that future data meets specifications. The process map in Exhibit 3.3 describes how a data request is initiated and validated.

As the data requests slow, this person becomes the Data Modeler. Already familiar with the data, he or she now understands

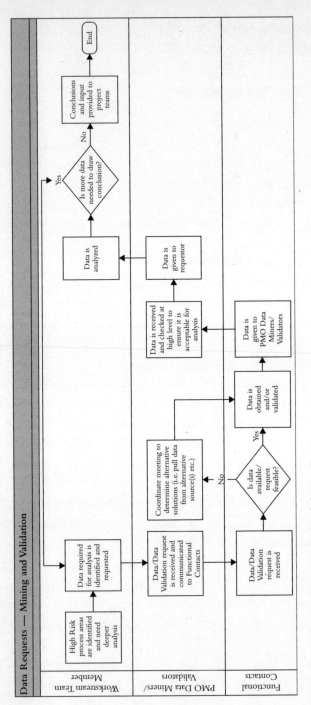

Exhibit 3.3 Data Mining and Validation Process

38

how to build standard reports that can be used across functions, operations, or the whole company. This person works closely with the Finance lead to ensure that the right data is being loaded into the metrics scorecards and business process management (BPM) dashboard. Matrix management is necessary, involving different functions and operations to build the metrics scorecard and BPM dashboard using the benchmarks already on hand or that the company will be purchasing. You can go as deep as you like to manage your process performance, but usually categories and Level 2 processes are sufficient. Categories capture the high-level functions that make up the business (e.g., sales/marketing, finance, human capital management, product development, production, etc.). Level 2 is all of the processes that roll up under the high-level categories. In the case of the Human Capital Management (category), the Level 2 processes might include HR Strategy and Planning, Recruiting and Staffing, Total Rewards, and the like. The American Productivity & Quality Center (APQC) has a very good taxonomy of business processes that you can use as a guide to line up against your processes. The taxonomy starts with strategy and ends with knowledge management, with each function and its associated activities represented in the framework. APQC also provides benchmarks, should you need them.

Change Management and Communications Lead

Every large project needs someone who oversees the change efforts and communicates them to employees. For Change Management, this lead is responsible for building a Change Management and Communications (CMC) plan with multiple channels, including a Pulse Survey to track employees' morale and productivity. Other responsibilities include development of mission and vision and key talking points for the CEO and leadership team and media relations. The CMC Lead must also allocate time to run communications for the project. In addition to connecting daily with PMO and weekly with workstream leads, this leader must understand how to communicate to the organization, especially to those directly affected by change. Being a proactive communicator helps the organization deal with adjustments and contributes to the maintenance of a well-focused work environment.

> **Quick Tip**
>
> ☞ If you don't have a good CMC resource in house, hire one on a contract basis to get the CMC workstream set up. They can work with the head of communications to set up a change management and communications strategy, then just advise you remotely. It should take about four to six weeks to setup the workstream and formulate the strategy and execution plan for the CEO and leadership team.

Workstream Leads

Workstream leads are the subject matter experts for a given discipline. They are responsible for detailed execution of the project plan as well as for the ability to think outside of the box. They connect daily with the workstream team and PMO and are usually the go-to people. They may need other resources part time to help with activities, but they are primarily the ones responsible for executing the project plan. There is tremendous collaboration between the workstreams, so forging a good team dynamic is crucial. As you'll see in Chapter 7, team dynamics play a big role in how a company performs.

The key to building a strong project team is to allocate your best people and allow them to focus solely on this project. Talk to their managers and move them out of their usual roles and into a department for Continuous Improvement. This is the first stage of moving to a culture that values and drives improving business performance.

One of the key success factors is to set goals for the team and link compensation to reward them for reaching targets and stretch goals. The core team's compensation is inextricably linked to performance, while only a portion of the Steering Committee's pay is linked to performance.

A sliding scale works best, so set three targets:

1. 95 percent of estimated savings
2. 100 percent of estimated savings
3. 110 percent of estimated savings

Only about 70 percent of the team's compensation should be directly tied to financials. The other 30 percent should be related to soft skills. Be communicative, resourceful, open-minded, and limitless . . . these attributes will tell you "how" the team got the work done. These roles should be considered growth opportunities for all involved, and a career path after the project ends will be important to keeping the team motivated. Have HR spend time with these people so they can be placed in the right role more easily after their tour of duty is over. Going back to their old role may not be possible. After the process is completed and the organization's structure has changed, it would be best to put them in a role that utilizes their newly acquired skills.

Equipping Your Team with the Necessary Tools

Now that you have a team to execute the playbook, you must set up the process and tools to run the project. You will need to have ready several standard tools before you start as well as processes that help the machine keep moving. The tools you will need are:

- Flexible project plan and tool
- Secure data repository and knowledge management database

- Data validation process
- Metrics dashboard
- Risk management database
- Financial models and tracking system
- Software: Visio, MiniTab, Webex
- Organizational Efficiency Tool kit
- Business Process Improvement Tool kit

First you need to detail the playbook using a *flexible project plan and tool*. It will better enable you and your team to transform the company. Although the playbook is complex, it can be managed quite efficiently using project management software. If you are working with external experts, they will set up the project plan for you. If you are doing it yourself, have a half-day session and just flesh out the work and the dates and come to an agreement on what the timeline will look like. The PMO operations team can get it into the right format and get it approved.

Quick Tip

☞ If you don't have MS Project, do not use MS Excel. It will require too much time for updating. Purchase enough MS Project licenses or online tools such as e-know's Integrator for the PMO Operations group to use.

Another important feature you'll need is a *secure data site* that will later link to your knowledge management database. Some companies use a shared drive; some contract with an external provider, such as Merrill, Linksys, or eRoom. Either way, the data site should be easy to use, offer the ability to upload a large amount of data, and have strong security settings. This is where you will house all documents related to the project. Version control will be important to maintain, so set up a naming convention that everyone can use when updating documents. The library you create should be searchable as well. Remember, the secure data site can transform into the knowledge management system. Once you move into the control stage of the project, remove all working documents from the site and have only final documents available for people to review.

Data validation will become a standard process during this project. A flawed data model will not deliver the right reports required to analyze the data. While the data model is being configured, you will need to pull the data for the teams and ensure that it is clean. Doing this requires looking up the source and confirming that the information is correct. Bad data in, bad data out.

As shown in Exhibit 3.3, there is a process for requesting data and validating it. The person who owns this will be building out the standard reports you will be using to load your metrics scorecard and the BPM dashboard.

You can begin to build your metrics scorecard and BPM dashboard using benchmarks you either already have or will be purchasing. You can go as deep as you like to manage your process performance, but usually Level 2 is sufficient. The metrics you choose now may not be the ones you ultimately end up tracking on in the dashboard, as the evolution of the project will determine which ones are right for the company to use. But you need to start somewhere, and the standard benchmarks are a good place.

Quick Tip

☞ If you aren't sure which metrics to start with, get external advice on what the most common three to four are within a function. They should include financial, organizational, customer, and operations metrics. 12 to 16 metrics company-wide is a good number to track; you shouldn't need more than that initially.

Although the metrics scorecard will track how the changes to the business are impacting business performance, risk management ensures that the business continues to move forward without suffering any major failures. If you don't have a risk management system, this is the time to build one. What function does this system play in the project and how important is it? VERY! Let me give you a real-life example of what happens when risk management fails.

My company was working on a restructuring effort for a technology manufacturing company, which had plants all over the world producing its products. As part of the project we conducted Lean Six Sigma reviews of the plants and scored them against standard metrics based on our observations. All of their plants were below average, but one plant in particular stood out as needing immediate intervention. The plant was in the process of implementing an enterprise-wide platform, which everyone thought was the answer to its productivity issues.

We had conducted a thorough review of the plant, spent a week there interviewing all the plant people, doing walk-arounds, and so on. What we found was that the people felt that they were not prepared to use the system, which was about to go live any day. The employees had not been trained sufficiently on the program, and they were very hesitant and nervous about the transition to the new system.

This was a huge red flag, so we went to the Risk Management Leader on the project team within one week of completing the assessment and asked for a meeting with the system team. The Risk Management Leader set up the meeting, and we reviewed our findings. When we asked what the contingency plan was, should there be issues, we were told by the system team leader that there wasn't one and that the company didn't need one. At that point, the Risk Management Leader—who also was an attorney at the company— should have demanded a plan B, documented it in the risk management system, set up a weekly status with the parties involved to ensure business continuity, and continued to track progress. This did not occur.

Three months later, the plant basically blew up. It went from shipping 400 products to 200 . . . ouch! Talk about a revenue killer. What was worse is that the Steering Committee and the PMO were aware of the problems, but because the CEO was not involved in the details, he did not know about this issue with the plant. He knew that the plant was in trouble, but he didn't know why. When we sat down with him to explain what had occurred and told him we had predicted this was going to happen, but no one took action to stop it, he was shocked. There is a lesson here; I hope you got it.

The most basic but hardest part to execute of the plan is the financial tracking and modeling that will be required. The tracking will be accomplished using a standard template that includes cost savings, revenue recognition, capital expenditure, severance payouts, and productivity gains. This should be updated weekly and reviewed with the Steering Committee, Restructuring Lead, and PMO Lead to track progress. A close connection to the controller's office is important for any call-outs that may occur.

The modeling of return on investment and cost/benefit analysis model will be required for any investments in technology, human capital, tools, and so on. You can use a standard model that your organization uses for other investments; if none exists, build one. Either way, this model should be the mechanism to help the Steering Committee decide what improvements or tools to prioritize.

The next set of tools you'll need are software tools: Visio, Minitab, and Webex. These are basic tools that you can buy and license out to whomever needs them within the organization. They are simple, inexpensive, and will drive the project team to greater productivity.

Visio is a standard process-mapping tool and is required for the Organization Efficiency (OE) and Business Process Improvement (BPI) workstream. At least one license is necessary for the team. Minitab is a statistical analysis tool used in Six Sigma and is required for the BPI team to run root cause analysis. You will need several licenses, depending on how many people will be doing the analysis. Webex is a standard communication tool for CMC and to share documents if you have people in different locations.

The OE and BPI tool kits are packages of tools and processes that you'll need to execute in the workstreams. We will talk in more detail about these deals in Chapter 6, but to the extent you can have some of the data and tools available, that will be a head start.

In order to conduct the OE analysis, you need a census run of your employee base and accurate organization charts. If the information is not accurate, start cleaning the data. Also, if you do not have up-to-date organization charts all the way down to the lowest level, start building them now. Getting the organization charts ready for when the OE workstream launches will save you time and effort later, and make the savings opportunities more accurate when you right size your organizations.

The BPI tool kit consists of mostly Six Sigma tools: fishbone diagrams, Pareto charts, drill-down trees, failure modes and effects analysis (FMEA), and so on. If you do not have Six Sigma in your company, or any Black Belts or Master Black Belts, we recommend you hire an external consultant. These are not methodologies and tools that just anyone can use. They take years of experience to master, and you must ensure the tools are being used properly.

Quick Tip

☞ Consider conducting Six Sigma training before you launch the project if you don't have this expertise in house. My firm has found that it is more productive to work with people who have been trained before project launch. Such people were more productive in executing the workstream activities and realizing savings and revenue.

We also found that explaining how to use the processes and tools was easier. Black Belt training takes about four weeks, and executive Six Sigma training takes about one week. Both are required as you move into a Continuous Improvement mind-set.

Now that you have set up the infrastructure for the project and have team members in place, they are ready to begin conducting a self-assessment and set the baseline for your current state. In Chapter 4, we review the approach your team will take to understand where you are and how far you need to go. You will now be moving from "Unconscious Incompetence" to "Conscious Incompetence."

Note

1. www.12manage.com/methods_raci.html.

Chapter 4

Setting the Baseline

Moving from Unconscious Incompetence to Conscious Incompetence

In Chapter 3, we talked about how important it is for you to know, as a business, where you are on the "Unconscious/Conscious" Continuum as well as what actions you need to take in order to move forward. Most companies find themselves in a situation where they don't know what they don't know, but even the ones with an adequate understanding of the problems are stumped when they consider where to begin fixing them. For this reason, performing a rigorous self-assessment is the first step toward helping you move into the next phase of the continuum. It is also the first step before you can effectively launch any restructuring effort because you must examine how well your business is functioning today against best-in-class (BIC) benchmarks.

An objective assessment using output metrics from your processes offers a complete view of your company's health, assuming the metrics directly link to your strategy. If they don't, you may be measuring the wrong things. A strategy road map that is linked to a balanced scorecard is the tool BIC companies use to monitor the state of their business. If you are missing one or both, or if they are not linked, you need to create them as soon as possible! If you have both but the balanced scorecard does not roll up to the strategy, you need to align them.

A strategy road map usually has five elements that are common to most companies. You can have more elements, but make sure they are truly things that are critical to your business. If you are not willing to put the effort into tracking an element, then it must not be absolutely critical to the running of your company. Even manual monitoring is better than nothing. The five common strategic elements are:

1. Improve operations quality and efficiency.
2. Grow through innovation and technology.
3. Increase customer satisfaction and retention.
4. Improve financial performance.
5. Empower the organization.

Within each of the strategic elements listed, more specific actions need to be implemented to impact the outcome. These actions are measured, and they are what make up the balanced scorecard. For example, a balanced scorecard action that would impact the first item, *improve operations quality and efficiency,* could be to become certified by the International Organization for Standardization (ISO) at all the manufacturing plants in the company or to make enterprise resource planning (ERP) the standard platform across the company. These changes are very easy to measure and track, and they clearly tie to the strategic element of improving operational quality and efficiency.

Another way to improve operational efficiency is through the use of systems and improved service from information technology (IT). This is where an IT balanced scorecard at the subprocess level is critical to meet the balanced scorecard action of improved service from IT. Later in this section, Exhibit 4.3 provides an example of an IT balanced scorecard.

A balanced scorecard action that ties to the third strategy road map element, increase customer satisfaction and retention, might be: Provide on-time warranty service personnel. For example, customers might say they are willing to wait up to 15 additional minutes after the scheduled time of service. If someone does not arrive within the 15 minutes, the metric would indicate that they were not on time, therefore impacting your customer satisfaction level. If you are able to provide personnel to a customer location for warranty repair or service on time, your satisfaction levels will increase, and that in turn will drive customer retention.

Our final example of a balanced scorecard action that ties to a strategic road map element is something that not all companies feel is important but is actually what differentiates great companies from good companies. It falls under the fifth strategic element, *empower the organization,* and involves the training and development of employees. Having a balanced scorecard action to "Provide the best training programs so our employees can be empowered," for example, goes a long way toward quicker decision making and employee-driven process improvements. This action could have projects under it that detail the types of training necessary to allow the employees to be empowered. For example, technical training empowers the employee to be a better service technician. Another project could be to train personnel on change acceleration program (CAP) and facilitation skills, which gives them tools to act in an empowered way.

Quick Tip

☞ Do not have more than six balanced scorecard actions per strategy road map element. More than six actions could mean you have gone one level too deep and are listing projects. Projects roll up to actions, so keep the actions high level, and list projects below them.

How many of the above elements do you have in place today? Do you have a strategy road map? Do you have a truly balanced scorecard, or does it just include a few financial and operational metrics? Do the elements in your strategic road map allow for detailed actions to be rolled up *and* measured to it? Do you have the governance and operational ability to track the scorecard and the projects? If you answered no to any of these questions, continue reading this chapter to learn how to create a true strategy road map and balanced scorecard.

To create a strategy road map, you must have current and relevant information on issues that impact your business. Most strategy road maps utilize analysis on the economy, environment, legal/regulatory, political, new technologies, and competitors. If you can understand in detail how each of these areas impacts your business, along with your own internal assessment of your strengths and weaknesses, you are well on your way to creating a strategy road map. A road map can be completed at both a company-wide level and a business-unit level, but be sure to link the business-level map to the overall company map, or you will have competing priorities. Exhibit 4.1 shows the most commonly used elements of a strategy road map.

Once everyone agrees on the elements for the strategy road map, it is time to create the actions that will be measured to ensure you are executing on your strategy. These measured actions become the balanced scorecard. If your systems cannot measure an

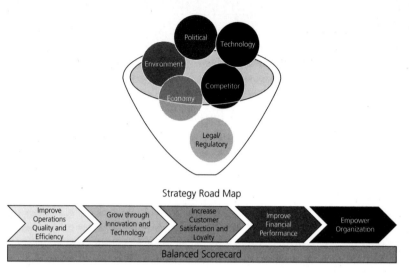

Exhibit 4.1   Strategy Road Map Funnel

action, then put a manual dashboard in place temporarily until you automate it. Just because you can't measure something doesn't mean it is removed from the scorecard. Exhibit 4.2 shows just one example of a strategic road map element and its associated balanced scorecard actions. Each scorecard action will have many projects that roll up into it. The action "Improve Service Level of IT Organization" requires a balanced scorecard for the IT organization to be developed and monitored. An example of a balanced scorecard for an IT organization at a major retailer is depicted in Exhibit 4.3. It is managed the same way as a company-wide scorecard, and each support function needs one because part of any function's role within the organization is to provide services to internal customers.

Converting strategy into measurable action items is critical to understanding your company's current state and helps you determine what your future state needs to be. It is an ongoing, iterative process that uses data to help guide your business and ensure project success both during and after the restructuring is completed.

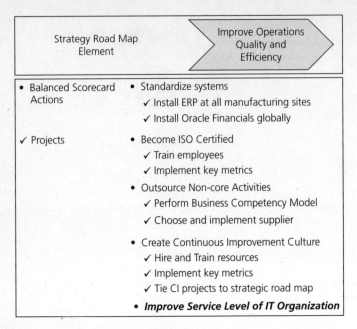

Exhibit 4.2   Strategy Road Map Element

You Are Here

Now that you have your strategy road map and balanced score-card, the next step is to do a self-assessment against benchmarks to see how you compare to BIC companies. Not all of the balance scorecard metrics are used. The restructuring self-assessment is a subset of the scorecard measurements with associated BIC benchmarks along with questions; together they indicate the current state. Only the subset of measurements and answers to key questions are necessary to determine the priorities and extent of restructuring needed. But the balanced scorecard continues to be used throughout the restructuring effort; now it becomes the method by which you monitor your processes long term as well as how you capture the impact of the changes that occur during the restructuring project.

Objective	Measure	Units	FY Target	Jan	Feb		Mar	
				Actuals	Target	Actual	Target	Actual
Business Value								
Control cost of IT	% investment vs. % maintainenance	%	50% or less Main.	39% Inv. 61% Main.	<50% Main.	43.4% Inv. 56.6% Main.	<50% Main.	48.7% Inv. 51.3% Main.
Maximize business unit value creations	Project portfolio NPV	No.	$30,000,000	1,123,908.29		3,793,327.23		13,191,000.34
User								
Keep systems running	% server uptime	%	97%	99.99%	97%	99.96%	97%	99.82%
Provide fast and predictable service delivery	% applications and services meeting SLAs	Weighted %	100%		90%		90%	
Meet user satisfaction needs	User satisfaction survey	Scale 1–10	6 out of 10	5.1	6	5.2	6	5.2
Offer innovations that provide business value	Approved projects orignating in IT	%	50%	24.50%	50%	12.50%	50%	26.60%
	% of IT budget spent on R&D	%	5%+/−1%	5.90%	5%	5.20%	5%	7.23%
Operational Excellence								
Process maturity	Management scorecard	No.	41		41	29	41	30
	#ITIL	No.	30		14	16	18	16
Provide secure systems	% of systems with approved security plan	%	100%	0%	0%	0%	0%	0%
	% of systems with approved disaster recovery plan	%	100%	0%	0%	0%	0%	0%
Manage projects effectively	Deviation of delivery date vs. plan	%	plus/minus 20% vs plan		20%	162.49%	20%	70.09%
	Project portfolio alignment vs. plan	%	90%	90%	90%	77.50%	90%	78.70%
Learning and Growth								
Hire and retain solid performers	Departmental turnover	%	10%	4.14%	1%	2.42%	1%	2.45%
	Employee satisfaction survey	Scale 1–10	9 out of 10	7.76				
	% of job role test completion	%	100%	4.30%	4.30%	4.30%	4.30%	4.30%
	% of IT budget spent on training	%	5%+/−1%	3.80%	Stable at 5%	5.70%	Stable at 5%	6.03%
Develop skills of existing staff	Degree of cross training (percentage of key skill sets covered by at least two people)	%	100%		100%	58%	100%	58%
Information capital	% of EAP complete	%	100%	0%	0%	0%	0%	0%
Promote culture of innovation	% of contributors to discussion board	%	100% participation	0%	100%	52%	100%	63%

NO VALUE

Exhibit 4.3   IT Balanced Scorecard

During a self-assessment, it is important not only to have the right data but to be honest about the outcome. You already agree you have to do something, otherwise you wouldn't be reading this book, so don't cheat yourself by thinking you are better than you are or that you are so different that these benchmarks don't apply to you. If the data says you are below benchmark in an area, don't try to convince yourself that you are better because "intuitively" you think you are. However, if the data says you are close to BIC, don't just assume you don't have more work to do in that area. There is always room for improvement. Companies that retain their best-in-class status are always changing or improving their processes. But for this effort, we are prioritizing the areas that are below benchmark, because there is an immediate need.

The Self-Assessment Scorecard (Exhibit 4.4) is divided into areas that make up the core activities of your company. If you are not currently measuring yourself against all of these benchmarks, you should be. Add them to your strategy road map immediately, and put a mechanism in place to start measuring. We assess nine areas:

1. Sales
2. Product development
3. Supply chain
4. Manufacturing
5. Customer satisfaction
6. Finance
7. Organization
8. Process
9. Technology

Here we only discuss the more unfamiliar benchmarks that you may not have in place today, since the others, such as finance indicators, are very common and easy to measure. As you can see from the exhibit, we outline some metrics to help you understand your current state. Although the list is not exhaustive, it reflects some relevant measures needed to conduct a comprehensive assessment.

Area	Metric	Best in Class	Baseline	Q1	Q2	Q3	Q4
Sales	Do you measure the business needs of your customers and share results?	Yes					
	Do you have a dedicated, collaborative sales forecasting software solution?	Yes					
	Are you linking financial incentives to forecasting accuracy?	Yes					
	Do you have a platform that allows the sales forecasts to be used for operations planning?	Yes					
Product Development	Do you have a differentiated supply chain for NPI?	Yes					
	Do you have dedicated supply chain engineers that work with the NPI engineers?	Yes					
	Do your product managers have end-to-end responsibility and accountability?	Yes					
	Do you utilize common parts of software code, located in a knowledge database?	Yes					
	How often do you meet your original launch date?	86%					
Supply Chain	Do you have a global, enterprise-wide system?	Yes					
	Are your systems solutions coordinated and multitiered?	Yes					
	Do you have risk management programs in place and service-level agreements (SLAs)?	Yes					
	Do you perform supply chain costing and analysis?	Yes					
	Have you implemented Lean methodologies?	Yes					
	Do you measure KPIs weekly?	Yes					
Manufacturing	Do you use Lean manufacturing methods?	Yes					
	Are you monitoring critical KPIs daily and less critical ones weekly?	Yes					
	Do you collaborate with customers and suppliers?	Yes					
	Do you have a global, integrated ERP system?	Yes					
	How often are you in compliance with your schedule?	94%					
	What is your average cycle time?	21 days					
	What is your raw material utilization?	97%					
	How often do you meet shipment or delivery dates?	97%					
Customer Satisfaction	How many net new customers gained do you have?	9% improvement					
	How much have you improved customer satisfaction?	9% improvement					
	How much have you grown market share?	10%+ improvement					
Finance	How much have you grown revenue?	9% improvement					
	How much have you increased profitability?	9% improvement					
Organization	How many layers do you have in your organization?	6					
	What is your average span of control?	10:01					
Process	How long does it take your leadership team to make an important decision?	10% improvement					
	How many decision makers have visibility to KPIs?	11% improvement					
Technology	Balanced scorecard based on strategy road map	Yes					
	Use of dashboard to access/monitor KPIs	Yes					
	Automated alerts and reports with autodistribution	Yes					
	Tool selection: ease of use, compatibility, and scalability	Yes					
	Enterprise-wide platforms implemented across organizations	Yes					

Exhibit 4.4 Self-Assessment Scorecard (all improvements are year-over-year)

How Fit Is Your Organization?

Why is it important to have an organization that is right sized, agile, and flexible? Because as today's macroeconomic issues squeeze sales and revenue, organizations need to focus on managing human capital better in order to maximize the productivity and value of each employee. An organization that is quick and nimble has the ability to change when opportunities or roadblocks appear. Whether the opportunities or roadblocks are competitive, environmental, or legal, an organization that can adapt quickly usually will succeed and win.

Some of the simplest metrics to track are organizational benchmarks. Conducting an organizational diagnostic assessment (ODA) every year should become part of what HR delivers to the Senior Leadership Team (SLT). An ODA comprises looking at the structure and metrics that provide the answers to how efficient the organization is and what gaps exist to getting to benchmark. Companies can review several metrics including payroll as a percentage of revenue, revenue generated per employee, and profit per full-time employee, but the two common metrics that tell the story the fastest are the number of layers in the organization and the average span of control.

Assessing these metrics is straightforward if your data is easy to access and is clean, accurate, and up to date. In general, the benchmarks are very basic, easy to understand, and are absolutely achievable. In my experience working with benchmark companies and being part of surveys to analyze BIC companies, any company, no matter how complex, big, or small, can achieve the benchmarks within 6 to 12 months.

What are the symptoms of companies whose organizations are inefficient?

- Decision making is slow due to too many layers and small spans of control.
- Managers "do the work" instead of managing people, yielding poor performance results.

- Many layers exist, with managers reporting to managers.
- "Promotional" opportunities result in small spans of control with managers leading only one or two people.
- Knowledge management is difficult to maintain due to legacy information deep in the trenches, making it difficult to retrieve and document.
- Employees are not empowered to make decisions due to a check-the-checker mentality.

An ODA is the first thing my firm does when we start a restructuring project. How do we do this? We get a data file from the client, which is an employee census, and we put it through a proprietary-developed tool. Once we have evaluated the data, we calculate the number of layers and the average span of control. Doing this manually will take a long time, especially if you are working off inaccurate organization charts. (We are talking about data again! Are you beginning to see how important clean accurate data is to understanding your business?)

Quick Tip

☞ If you can, hire an external resource to do the ODA for you the first time. Learn how to use the tool so that you can do it the following year and on a continual basis thereafter. The results will be more accurate and faster if you can use an automated tool. Also, the leadership team will be more willing to accept the outcome if they know it was from a neutral party.

To build the census, the data file should include:

- Employee identity
- Job title
- Supervisor

- Grade (if you have them)
- Salary (broken out by base, bonus, other)
- Business or function
- Location

We count the number of layers starting with the CEO (layer 1) and going all the way down to the last layer. The benchmark is 6 layers.[1] Most companies have at least 8 to 10; some even have 11. That's almost double the benchmark! Imagine how long it takes for decisions to be made and how much micromanagement is occurring.

A funny story can show you how out of touch senior management can be about the details of the company or even the business unit. Remember the company I talked about in Chapter 3, whose plant basically blew up? We were at a leadership meeting with 70 of the company's top managers (basically the top two layers of the organization). We were there to talk about the restructuring initiative that it was undertaking. We had just finished the ODA and identified 11 layers in the organization. The CEO had communicated this to his Senior Leadership Team prior to the meeting. During the leadership meeting, one of his direct reports came up to me while I was speaking to the head of HR and said, "So which group has the 11 layers?" I smiled and said, "Yours does." The leader seemed shocked, and said it was impossible. My response was "Data does not lie . . . intuitive analysis does. When was the last time you did an analysis of layers?" The answer: "Never."

I will say, of all the leaders in the company, this person was the most proactive about getting the organization in shape, much more so than anyone else who sat on the Steering Committee.

Now let's talk about spans of control, or SoC. Benchmarks are calculated for the overall enterprise and by functional area. For example, in sales and customer service (call centers or field service) the SoC is much larger. They manage anywhere from 15 to 20, and growing. It is common to see a great manager with a span of 24 to 30. We also see high numbers in a shared service environment, such as benefits administration or finance and accounting.

Exhibit 4.5 shows average SoCs for any given layer. However, as I said, each function and business segment is different. Typically, anything under 6 is poor, but this number is still small and begs the question: What is the value of having a 1:6 ratio? In my experience, the better the leader, the more people he or she is managing. Companies with good leadership training programs typically have the best SoCs.

My firm is currently working on updating the Organization Efficiency benchmarks by conducting a Global Organization Efficiency Survey (GOES) on layers and spans. By the time this book is published, the benchmarks will change. My hypothesis is that with the

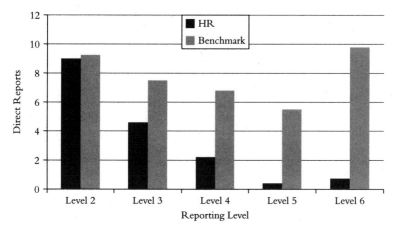

	HR	Benchmark
Level 2	9	9.25
Level 3	4.6	7.5
Level 4	2.2	6.8
Level 5	0.4	5.5
Level 6	0.75	9.8

Exhibit 4.5 Organizational Diagnostic Assessment

> **Quick Tip**
>
> ☞ If you have SMEs who excel at their craft or are incredibly good at their function, do not make them managers. A managerial position will distract them from their core competency and focus them on something they may not be good at. Look for good people managers, not experts, to manage large groups.

increasing use of technology and remote workforces, the SoC's numbers will increase. As companies become leaner, people will take on larger groups of people to manage, and technology will enable it to occur.

Now let's move from people to processes and look at BIC benchmarks for the key processes in your company.

How Robust Are Your Processes?

We just finished looking at the people in your organization and how to determine if your company is right sized. Now we are going to look at the processes that support the people, to see how robust they are by comparing them to BIC benchmarks. Are you using the newest technologies, do you utilize customer input, and have you built in quality with metrics that monitor your processes? If we look at sales, simple yes-or-no answers help us determine where you stand compared to BIC. As you encounter barriers in the market, either from economic or competitive pressures, the customer becomes the critical player in achieving BIC status. Understanding the needs of your customers, measuring those needs, implementing changes based on those needs and communicating back to the customer, via a robust feedback channel, on the results of the improvements is something that companies rarely do, but it is incredibly important.

If you can show customers that what they want is important to you, they will view even small improvements positively. To do this, you must have technology not just to track the customers' needs but also to help you forecast and plan, so there are no surprises for you or your customers. An important question to ask yourself is: Do we have a dedicated, collaborative sales forecasting software solution? Many companies capture actual sales but don't have software that can be used in collaboration with customers to determine both short- and long-term forecasts. If you do have this type of system, are you linking financial incentives to forecasting accuracy? Doing this forces the organization to hone forecasting skills either with new software updates or better customer interaction. Do you have a platform that allows the sales forecasts to be used for operations planning? If you answer no to any of these questions, issues farther downstream probably are the result of a lack of technology and customer involvement at the beginning of the process. Let's look at the next area, product development.

Product development is typically the core of what any company does. Every company has a product development organization regardless of whether it sells products or services. How quickly products or services are introduced is the most important element of product development. BIC companies hit launch dates 86 percent of the time compared to the original launch date and bring products to market 25 percent faster than all other companies.[2] This is not an adjusted launch date, which businesses frequently use to measure themselves. Don't fool yourself into thinking you are best in class if the launch date changes! You may be sitting there saying "But my parts got caught up in customs and I can't control that so I had to change the launch date." No! You *do* have control over that issue. If you have an adequate risk management program in place that can predict potential issues and have action plans in place to quickly react when issues do arise, then the issue no longer exists.

BIC companies have a differentiated supply chain just for new product introductions (NPI) with weekly supply chain management reviews. Do you have these in place? Do you have dedicated supply chain engineers who work with the NPI engineers to ensure the right parts with the right specifications are sourced correctly the first time? If you have answered no to any of these questions, you are at a competitive disadvantage and are spending more money than necessary to introduce and produce your products. You probably have issues in both your supply chain and manufacturing operations, all originating from your product development process.

Speaking of supply chain . . . how automated is your process? Is it a global, enterprise-wide system? Are your systems solutions coordinated and multitiered? Do you have risk management programs in place for suppliers that have shown problems in the past or that are deemed high risk? Do you perform supply chain costing and analysis? Have you implemented Lean methodologies? Are you tracking key performance indicators (KPIs) on a weekly basis?

Many of you will be answering no to these questions, but if you are answering yes, you are way ahead of the curve. Most BIC companies have implemented all of the items just listed. But average and below-average companies are just now beginning to understand supply chain and how to manage it. It may seem overwhelming to implement a global, enterprise-wide system that takes years to complete, but it is one of the key drivers impacting outcomes that show up in the manufacturing process and other areas, such as product quality, on-time delivery, and cost. Therefore, it is critical to get your supply chain processes and technology up to par; otherwise, you may have to fix issues farther downstream in manufacturing or as part of your customer service/warranty repair process.

So let's talk about manufacturing. This is where many issues become visible even though they were created farther upstream. But issues internal to manufacturing can be prevented by using BIC methods. The first question is: Do you use Lean manufacturing methods? If you answered no, stop everything and start working on this immediately. All BIC companies use some form of Lean manufacturing along with KPIs that are monitored real time on a daily basis. Those metrics include product quality, throughput, scheduling compliance, and on-time shipments. BIC companies typically institute Six Sigma programs along with Lean, so their product quality is exceptional. But even if Six Sigma has not been implemented, BIC companies still adhere to their schedules 94 percent of the time, with completed and on-time shipments at 97 percent.[3]

Other measurements that can be monitored weekly, such as manufacturing costs, show a significant difference between average and BIC companies, running typically 13 percent less (53 percent versus 40 percent of revenue), while cycle time has a 5-day differential with BIC companies at 21 days while average companies are in the 26-day range.[4] Where do you fit into these measurements? Are you even measuring these attributes? If you are, how do you compare? Earlier I mentioned the importance of customer interaction and input. Does your manufacturing team collaborate with customers and suppliers? Do you have systems, such as ERP, that are globally integrated?

Process metrics indicate how well your organization is running from an administrative standpoint. That is why the two key metrics under process are "time to decision" and "space of decision makers with visibility to KPIs."

The time it takes to make decisions can be a huge advantage in many ways. Organizations that go into analysis paralysis will always be the followers; those that can make quick decisions become the leaders. These leading companies usually have exceptional data management systems, which allow them to have complete trust in their decisions and the potential outcomes.

How do you track something as ambiguous as decision making? One way we have found to do this at the senior level is as part of the balanced scorecard.

For example, perhaps a decision needs to be made regarding opening a new service location in XYZ city. The date that it is brought before the CEO or SLT is the initiation date; the completion date and difference in days is not filled in; and

> **Quick Tip**
>
> ☞ Build an action register. Add to the next page of your balanced scorecard an action register with all action items that are on your agenda for your weekly Senior Leadership Team (SLT) staff meetings and any items that get added to it during the meeting. These columns are necessary: There should be a column that tracks the "date of initiation"; the next column tracks the "date of completion," followed by a "difference in days" column; and the last column tracks any "follow-up" necessary. An easy way to view status is by adding a column that displays a red (will not meet deadline), yellow (potential issues with meeting deadline) or green (on track to meet deadline) circle next to each action item.

the follow-up would list "do a cost/benefit analysis on the location." When the cost/benefit analysis is done and brought before the CEO or SLT, and a yes/no decision is made, then the completion date can be filled in. The difference between the two dates should be calculated in days. Total the difference in days at the bottom of the sheet(s); this becomes your current state "time to decision" figure. Each week you should update the columns with new projects and completion dates with the total at the bottom of the page. This becomes your week-over-week comparison. If this process becomes too cumbersome, you can still track the dates each week but do the comparison only for the month. Each week or month you should see an improvement on the time to decision metric, with a year-over-year improvement of 10 percent.[5]

Time to decision is just one of the key metrics the SLT should be seeing on a weekly basis. The entire balanced scorecard should be reviewed weekly, but in detail only for high-risk areas. Remember, these measurements are the pulse of your organization, so taking the time to review the results of the scorecard and understand why something is trending up or down will help you run your company effectively.

To calculate the number of KPIs to which the SLT has visibility, count the number of KPIs you review at your SLT meetings. That is your current-state figure. As you initiate projects that tie to your balanced scorecard, you will have greater visibility into the core issues based on the metrics you capture. Add this metric to your current balanced scorecard so you can see how many you currently have visibility to as well as how you progress as you implement a more detailed balanced scorecard.

Now comes the important part. Share the results with your entire organization so each and every employee can be on the same page as the SLT. Having everyone understand the measurements and how each person is impacted by the results goes a long way toward teamwork. This is why it is so important not only to know the number of KPIs you are tracking but also to know how many decision makers have visibility to them. In the end, every person in your organization should see and understand the KPIs. It takes time to do this. A one-time e-mail to all employees in an organization doesn't count. People must be trained to understand what KPIs measure, how it is being measured, and what the result of the measurement means both to the company and to them. Finally, having everyone understand what the outcome needs to be and how to achieve it is the most critical part of the communication. BIC companies see an 11 percent year-over-year improvement in the number of decision makers with visibility to KPIs, but even a few percent a year is progress and will have a positive impact.[6]

If you are not measuring these process metrics, or if you are but are not best in class, the first thing you should do is add them to your balanced scorecard. Start measuring your processes now. Once the restructuring effort starts, you will need to make quick decisions based on data. If you are too slow, you will stall the effort and create doubt in your employees' minds.

Being objective and honest about where you stand relative to best in class is an important piece of the assessment. It helps you prioritize your restructuring efforts and build the balanced scorecard measurements that are necessary to track throughout the project and beyond. How did you do? Are there areas that stand out as needing immediate attention?

Now it's time to look at how to tailor your restructuring effort to address immediate needs, along with a long-term holistic approach to restructure and revamp your entire business. This initiative will be critical to the speed and extent of success of your restructuring, and will be how the business operates for a few years, so take time to do it right.

Notes

1. Ron Nicol, "Shaping Up: The Delayered Look," Boston Consulting Group, 2004.
2. The Lean Product Development Benchmark Report, Aberdeen Group, May 2007.
3. Cindy Jutras, The Manufacturing Performance Management Benchmark Report, Aberdeen Group, June 2006.
4. Ibid.
5. A benchmark study by Aberdeen Group, a Harte-Hanks company, cosponsored by Dundas, iDashboards, Insightformation, Corda, and Actuate, Aberdeen Group, October 17, 2007.
6. Ibid.

Chapter 5

Ready to Launch

Kicking Off Your Restructuring Project

In Chapter 4, we laid out the importance of the strategy road map and balanced scorecard in order to set the baseline for what the business will need to achieve. However, these items are two dimensional and are only as good as the organization that executes them. What is the organization's role in the success of a business? How do you create a valuable organization? The answer is by sharing resources and knowledge. When you do this, you develop an organization whose sum is greater than its parts and whose costs are spread across the enterprise. This includes external vendors and suppliers as well. The value of the restructuring project comes from the reduced costs the organization contributes to the bottom line. But achieving this is easier said than done.

By now you've assembled a Steering Committee and project team that will undertake the mission of executing a restructuring program and fundamentally changing the way you operate, helping create the value the customer and shareholders expect. You have committed your time to make sure the program has the exposure and support from the Senior Leadership Team (SLT) and board of directors. Now it's time to put the playbook into action and officially launch the initiative.

When we start a project with a client, we conduct a three-day launch session. We spend two days with the project team, followed by a third day with the Steering Committee and SLT, including the CEO. The goal of the launch meeting is to ensure that everyone is on the same page with regard to the balanced scorecard, the project plan activities and timing, communications strategy, financial goals to achieve, and the roles and responsibilities of each group.

The first- and second-day agenda should include:

- Review of assessment and opportunities
- Stakeholders analysis
- Elevator speech
- Execution of templates
  a. Project Management Office (PMO) operations
     i. Forms: Status updates form, data request forms, travel and expense forms, etc.
     ii. Tools: Knowledge database, Microsoft Project, Minitab, etc.
  b. Risks, mitigants and interdependencies
  c. Goals and objectives forms
- Breakouts for workstreams
  a. RASCI model
  b. Planning of activities and timeline

The third-day agenda should include:

- Review of assessment and opportunities
- Burning platform
- Stakeholder analysis review

- Elevator speech review
- Risks and mitigants factors Interdependencies

Because the PMO is responsible for compiling the information that will be shared at the meeting, it is the first group to be trained on the tools, templates, and processes that will be used. The next list describes the templates that should be completed during the meeting and updated on a regular basis.

- **Burning platform.** A statement from the CEO explaining "why" the restructuring program is necessary and how important it is to the business.
- **Elevator speech.** Short, concise paragraph outlining what the program is about and how you will achieve your goals.
- **Stakeholder analysis.** This should include all stakeholders, starting with the board of directors, CEO, SLT, managers, and employees as well as external stakeholders like Wall Street analysts and investors.
- **Risks and mitigants.** List of risks associated with the restructuring program and mitigants to ensure they do not occur. Risk management owns this list and keeps it up to date weekly.
- **Interdependencies.** Activities or elements of the playbook that are dependent on variables like information technology (IT) investments, other processes being improved, and so forth.
- **RASCI model.** Review of ownership of activities and tasks for execution of Playbook.

Before any templates are completed, the project team examines a full review of the assessment and opportunities and confirms goals for each workstream. Typically, the project team fills in the templates during the first day of the session and then shares them with the SLT to get input before finalizing them. An external resource should facilitate this session if possible, in order to help the team think creatively. The Communications Leader plays a big role in these meetings, as this person is the one who will use the outputs as content in the change management strategy for the stakeholders. Once team members understand and agree on the assessment and opportunities, they need to fill out a stakeholders' analysis to see what they are up against. Exhibit 5.1 is an example of a typical stakeholders' analysis.

There will always be resisters, people who openly communicate their nonsupport of the effort, and there are those who will hide behind a smile and words, even though they secretly do not support the effort either. These are the ones to be careful of, as they will try to sabotage the effort. Experience tells me that the most senior levels in the company are the resistors. I remember something told to me by one of my clients, a very strong CEO, who said this about those who sabotage: "It's like a disease . . . you need to seek it out and remove it from the organization." And he did. Half his SLT was replaced within 18 months, replaced by higher-quality talent, mostly from outside the company. The key in change management is to move the resistant stakeholders from a negative position to a neutral position at least; at best, to a positive position where they support the initiative.

Stakeholder	Positive	Neutral	Negative	Risk to Success
Board of Directors	X			Medium
CEO	X			High
SLT		X	X	Medium
Managers			X	Medium
Employees		X		High
Customers		X		Low
External (analysts, vendors, etc)			X	Low

Exhibit 5.1 Stakeholders' Analysis

The project team shares the stakeholders' analysis with the CEO and SLT on the third day. There may be some negative reaction if the project team has identified the SLT as negative or neutral. That's okay. The resisters need to know that they aren't fooling anyone with their lip service.

The next step in the stakeholders' analysis is when the Restructuring Lead meets with the CEO separately. Together they analyze each SLT member and create a plan to deal with unsupportive members. If these people don't become supporters in one quarter, it's time for the CEO either to have a heart-to-heart about the penalties for not being aligned with the rest of the organization or simply to replace them.

> **Quick Tip**
>
> ☞ Taking actions against resisters makes a statement, and you need to complete the actions quickly to set a precedent. If not, the rest of the organization will think going against the initiative is okay and that there will be no repercussions. Be swift, and make changes as soon as you need to.

Once you complete the stakeholders' analysis, and you know the issues, the CMC Lead takes this input and creates a change strategy for each stakeholder group. We will talk more about the CMC strategy in the upcoming chapters.

The next step is to create an elevator speech, a short, concise paragraph describing your mission and vision for what the company wants to achieve and what the restructuring initiative entails. It should be something that every employee in the company can remember and recite, so it needs to be short and simple. Again, this works best if you have an external resource who knows how to construct an elevator speech and is versed in change management and restructuring. An example might be similar to the one shown in Exhibit 5.2.

To execute our strategy and move rapidly to take advantage of quickly expanding market opportunities, XYZ has launched a restructuring initiative programmed to fundamentally change the way we operate. We will become more customer focused and market driven, reducing redundancies and process inefficiencies and freeing up significant funds to invest in technology and growth areas. We will engage employees in this initiative because our employees are crucial to our continued growth and success. Our goals are to evolve into a company that is simpler to do business with, more innovative, fast moving and entrepreneurial, able to scale quickly and move rapidly to take advantage of opportunities in the market. We will drive toward increasing revenue growth and higher profit margins to our shareholders, and make XYZ a great place to work, with opportunities for interesting, robust careers that will inspire you to be the best you can be.

Exhibit 5.2   Elevator Speech

You share the elevator speech with the CEO and SLT on the third day, tweaking it with any language or points they would like to include. It then gets handed off to the Communications Leader to distribute in whatever form or channel chosen.

The next task is to review and complete the templates and get trained on the tools (basic documents and tools for operating a project). I won't go into detail about the PMO operations tools and forms, because I discussed them in Chapter 3. You may use ones that are different from the ones shown. If you don't know whether you have them, ask human resources and IT; they should have most of these forms. An important, mandatory template is the risks, mitigants, and interdependencies form. For every risk identified, you must have a mitigant, an action or plan to remedy the risk, and an owner for that risk. This ensures that the high-level risks are addressed and maintained for the CEO and SLT update meetings. This form is shared on the third day and then finalized. Once finalized, the form is given to the risk management team to manage on a weekly basis. The Restructuring Lead takes any risks that go "red" to the Steering Committee and the CEO immediately for help in mitigating their impacts.

The last task for the project team is to break out into separate workstreams and plan the activities around the project plan as well as complete the RASCI model. This is essential to make sure that the team members know what their roles and responsibilities are and link them to their goals and objectives. Since their performance will be rated based on their accomplishments from the project, it's crucial they know what they are expected to deliver and when. The status update document will be the means for tracking on-time delivery of the project activities and will be a way for the Restructuring Lead to rate the project team members. Exhibit 5.3 is an example of a simple status update you can use for each workstream.

The one task for which the CEO and SLT are solely responsible is the burning platform. They must come up with the reason they are launching the restructuring program and the importance of doing it *now*. This platform will provide the main talking points for the CEO to communicate consistently to all the employees and board of directors.

Communicating this one time is not enough. Reinforcing the message over and over at town hall meetings, Webcasts, and e-mails will help strengthen the case for change and emphasize the significance this initiative will have on the future success of the company. (See Exhibit 5.4 for an example.)

Do not officially launch the project until you have had the three-day alignment session and finalized the elevator speech and the burning platform.

Typically, the CEO announces the project in a forum that is open to all employees. E-mail is *not* an option. Use a Webcast, broadcast voicemail, town hall meeting, anything that will allow the CEO to "speak" to the employees. Use the burning platform as the basis for the project, identify a future state, and then introduce the team that will enable the execution of activities. As I mentioned, being open and honest is the best way to get the organization behind you. Not every employee will be happy to hear that change will occur, and many employees will have a lot of uncertainty, but keeping communication channels open will help calm the fears in the organization and breed trust.

Workstream	Status	Accomplishments This Week	Tasks for Next Week	Owners	Issues/Notes
Organizational Design	G	» Reviewed activity survey findings and executive interview fishbone analyses » Scheduled process mapping sessions > Dates, times, and venues are set > Invitations sent to all invitees with copies to management > Declined invitations are being routed to functional department heads for replacement > At this writing, 63 invitations sent, 46 accepted, 2 declined » Friday conference call	» Monday conference call » Ongoing adjustments to process mapping schedule » Friday conference call	» NexGen » Tim » Bob	» Need to direct video conference technicians as to setup for process mapping » TI session involves participants; P. Wright requesting detailed agenda so they can "come and go" via video as needed

Status Key: **G** = on track   **Y** = caution/needs attention   **R** = needs urgent action

Exhibit 5.3   Status Update, Week of June 16, 2008

Exhibit 5.4   Burning Platform

Few people are willing to go on a journey without knowing where they're going, and it's no different for XYZ Associates. In June, we asked them to "set out on the road to a new way of life at XYZ." Now, weeks later, we're long overdue in sharing with them and you what lies at the end of the highway—especially since we expect them to travel it with us.

This overview is intended to provide you with an analysis of why change is needed at XYZ and how we intend to—once again—dominate the marketplace.

Let's start with the state of our business. We are the market leader in many of our businesses, and that's something to be proud about. Yet our market share has been declining, profit margins have dropped, and operating expenses are up. XYZ's financial performance has been disappointing and lags the overall market. Obviously, something isn't right.

Over the past five years:

- *Revenue growth averaged 5.2% per year, while our operating income growth rate was a low 2.2%.*
- *Margins have declined from 12.6% to 10.9%.*
- *The share price for our common stock in November 2006 was virtually the same as it was five years earlier—yet the overall market increased over 20% during those five years, and the share price of many peer companies more than doubled.*
- *We're growing at 3% annually, while best-in-class companies have grown at a rate of 50%.*
- *Some of our businesses have lost market share, either to large national competitors or local independents.*

Why has this happened? Without a doubt, some external factors are responsible—such as increased regulatory restrictions, changes in consumer sentiment and behavior, and rising costs, including fuel, employee health insurance, and interest rates. Regardless, we should have responded better.

As business units, we haven't performed to expectations. As functions, we have not done our best to serve our customers—the business units—to support their success. And although we may not agree on what went wrong specifically, we all bear responsibility. Yet there is universal agreement on one key point: Our future at XYZ will be different. Here's why:

Cost Structure

Our cost structure keeps us from being nimble—from making quick adjustments on the fly—when we're faced with rising costs. Empowering the businesses to make cost decisions and, when needed, to take calculated risks for the good of our customers will be our goal.

In addition, we need to share information up, down, and across the organization. Communications must improve so those closest to the customer can make informed decisions and have the greatest impact on business success.

Customer Focus and Growth

We are not prioritizing our efforts on doing the right things. There has been too much time spent on internally driven tasks that distract our front-line associates from doing what matters most—and that which adds value for customers and differentiating our products and services from the competition.

Bureaucracy

It's no secret that our business/corporate functions are misaligned. Conflict and confusion can no longer be tolerated. Nor can we tolerate bureaucracy, which is fostered by unneeded management layers between those associates whose work directly affects our customers and our leadership. As you know, we've already started to take action in this area.

Change at XYZ has been rumored to include plans to outsource, reduce headcount, cut costs, and more. Frankly, we don't yet know how the plan will be designed. But we do know this: Every business and function must be focused first on generating revenue and serving customers for XYZ to continue to grow and maintain its market share. To that end, the functions that support our businesses will, in the future, exist solely to help those businesses be successful.

It means that we will adopt a new mindset around how we deliver support activities. Together, the businesses and our functions—as partners—will determine what is needed and how it should be delivered—all with the idea of generating efficiencies, quality, and cost savings. Outsourcing is a possibility in some cases but not certainty in every situation. Better service, higher quality, and less cost are determining factors in our decisions.

The road we're traveling is bumpy. Yet it is one that we must take because if we do not transform ourselves into a leaner, more agile company—someone else will do it for us. That's a road trip none of us wants to take.

Exhibit 5.4 (*Continued*)

> *When we reach the end of our journey, the rewards will be apparent. We will be stronger, more efficient, and more profitable. We will be the envy of our competitors. The most talented people in the world will vie to work here. The savviest investors will bet on our continued success. And we will have the satisfaction of knowing that it was our commitment and passion to reach excellence that made it happen.*
>
> *This intiative is more than mere change. It is a revolution in how we do business with our customers and with ourselves. We have nothing but the utmost confidence in the people of XYZ to make it happen.*

Exhibit 5.4   (*Continued*)

So You Think You Can Change?

Fear of change is the one factor that will prevent you from improving your organization. We have already discussed the need for a rigorous change management and communications strategy in Chapter 3, but how much do you really know about it? What exactly does change management mean? The definition we use says:

> Change management is the process during which the changes of a system are implemented in a controlled manner by following a predefined framework/model with, to some extent, reasonable modifications.[1]

If we break the definition apart, we can better understand the relevance of each point.

- "The process during which the changes to a system are implemented." For restructuring, the "process" is the project plan and the "system" is the business.
- "In a controlled manner by following a predefined framework. A "controlled manner" is through a project team with governance structure, including a Steering Committee.
- "Predefined framework" is the restructuring model we started with in Chapter 1.

So if you have all the change management components in order, then getting the organization aligned should be easy, right?

WRONG!!!! Change has been difficult to manage since 513 B.C. when Heraclitus of Greece stated: "There is nothing permanent except change." An even more profound Niccolò Machiavelli stated in the sixteenth century in *The Prince*: "There is nothing more difficult to take in hand, more perilous to conduct, or more uncertain in its success, than to take the lead in the introduction of a new order of things." This should resonate with anyone who has tried to implement change.

Change management entails thoughtful planning, sensitive implementation, and, above all, consultation with and involvement of the people affected by the changes. If you force change on people, problems arise. Change must be realistic, achievable, and measurable. When putting your change management and communications strategy together, you should ask yourself several questions:

- What do we want to achieve with this change, why, and how will we know that the change has been achieved?
- Who is affected by this change, and how will they react to it?
- How much of this change can we achieve ourselves, and what parts of the change do we need help with?

Additionally, you can adopt several principles to help you think through the CMC strategy. I like John P. Kotter's *Eight Steps to Successful Change*.[2] Kotter suggests that for change to be successful, 75 percent of a company's management needs to buy in to the change. This is why the stakeholders' analysis for your SLT must be conducted and actions must be taken if they are not supportive and acting as change advocates. Kotter's model conveys people's response and approach to change, in which people *see, feel* and then *change*. Kotter's eight steps include:

1. Establish a sense of urgency.
   a. Examine market and competitive realities.
   b. Identify and discuss crises, potential crises, or major opportunities.

2. Form a powerful guiding coalition.
   a. Assemble a group with enough power to lead the change effort.
   b. Encourage the group to work as a team.
3. Create a vision.
   a. Create a vision to help direct the change effort.
   b. Develop strategies for achieving that vision.
4. Communicate the vision.
   a. Use every vehicle possible to communicate the new vision and strategies.
   b. Teach new behaviors by the example of the guiding coalition.
5. Empower others to act on the vision.
   a. Get rid of obstacles to change.
   b. Change systems or structures that seriously undermine the vision.
   c. Encourage risk taking and nontraditional ideas, activities, and actions.
6. Plan for and create short-term wins.
   a. Plan for visible performance improvements.
   b. Create those improvements.
   c. Recognize and reward employees involved in the improvements.
7. Consolidate improvements and produce still more change.
   a. Use increased credibility to change systems, structures, and policies that don't fit the vision.
   b. Hire, promote, and develop employees who can implement the vision.
   c. Reinvigorate the process with new projects, themes, and change agents.
8. Institutionalize new approaches.
   a. Articulate the connections between the new behaviors and organizational success.
   b. Develop the means to ensure leadership development and succession.

A strong CMC plan, like the one in Exhibit 5.5, will address all eight of these steps as well as consider the means by which you will execute them. Various channels of communication will be important to ensure you reach every stakeholder. Also, the communication channels are different depending on who is delivering the message. The CEO may use a different form of communication from the SLT, as you the next examples show. Because the CEO Champions the restructuring program, he or she needs to deliver more communications to the entire audience, using different channels.

The leadership team will have a similar plan that addresses the groups this team manages. Although the form of communication may be different, but members of this team should incorporate the elevator speech and the burning platform in their key messages.

Another important document to develop and maintain with new input is a list of questions and answers. These can be put on a Web site or e-mailed. The SLT can use these questions and answers to educate managers on what to say when asked about the restructuring program in order to ensure that a consistent and accurate message is conveyed throughout the organization. Some sample Q&As are:

Q: Am I going to lose my job?
A: At this point, the company is analyzing all aspects of its operations and processes and evaluating employee performance in all of our businesses and countries. We will communicate as soon as possible after final decisions are made.

Q: Will there be one date when all layoff decisions will be communicated?
A: No. There are several different reviews taking place, and they will not be completed at the same time.

Q: Will employees who lose their jobs be given severance or early retirement options, if they are eligible?
A: There will be severance for employees whose jobs are eliminated, and we are considering options such as early retirement.

Month	Jan	Feb	Mar	Apr	May	Jun	Jul	Aug	Sep	Oct	Nov	Dec
Objective	Year-End Business Results	SBA and BOS	Employee Sat	Q1 Results /Skip Levels	Employee Devel.	Employee Sat.	Mid-Yr Business Results	Innovation and Improvement	Employee Sat.	Q3 Results	Business Planning	End-of-Year Accomplishments
Stakeholder												
BOD and Analysts				▪ Update BOD at board meeting ▪ Update analysts on earnings call			▪ Update BOD at board meeting ▪ Update analysts on earnings call			▪ Update BOD at board meeting ▪ Update analysts on earnings call		
BOD and Senior Leaders	▪ Off-site leadership meeting ▪ Build SBA and BOS	▪ SMT meeting	▪ Pulse survey	▪ MOR ▪ Skip levels with VPs	▪ 360 surveys	▪ Pulse survey	▪ MOR ▪ Webcast	▪ Off-site leadership meeting ▪ Identify top 5 ideas from workout and webchat	▪ Pulse survey	▪ MOR ▪ Webcast	▪ BP review meeting with senior leaders	▪ Dinner and celebration with senior leaders ▪ Pulse survey
High Potentials	▪ Webcast	▪ Town hall	▪ Pulse survey	▪ Skip levels ▪ Webcast	▪ 360 surveys	▪ Pulse survey	▪ Webcast	▪ Workout with HiPo's, report out to CEO and SVP's	▪ Pulse survey	▪ Webcast	▪ E-mail from CEO on goals	▪ Reward and recognition through Web site or e-mail ▪ Pulse survey
Employees < 2yrs service	▪ Webcast	▪ Town hall	▪ Pulse survey	▪ Webcast	▪ 360 surveys	▪ Pulse survey	▪ Webcast	▪ Web chat with CEO, SVP's of RAC/ HERC/ Europe	▪ Pulse survey	▪ Webcast	▪ E-mail from CEO on goals	▪ Reward and recognition Web site or e-mail ▪ Pulse survey
Employee Workforce	▪ Webcast	▪ Town hall	▪ Pulse survey	▪ Webcast	▪ 360 surveys	▪ Pulse survey	▪ Webcast	▪ Web chat with CEO, SVP's	▪ Pulse survey	▪ Webcast	▪ E-mail from CEO on goals	▪ Reward and recognition through Web site or e-mail ▪ Pulse survey

Exhibit 5.5 CEO Restructuring Communications Calendar

We are reviewing all severance-related issues at the same time as we are conducting analyses that could result in job reductions. The goal will be to treat employees who lose their jobs as humanely and professionally as possible and to communicate decisions effectively.

Q: What kinds of reviews could result in layoffs?

A: Overall, the effort is focused on organizing the company so it can operate as efficiently as possible. Department budgets have been streamlined to reduce costs and focus on essential activities. The organizational structure of the company is being reviewed with the goal of eliminating bureaucracies and redundancies and promoting better teamwork. That goal will be achieved in part by delayering the organization and also reviewing individual employee performance. Also, we are reviewing which jobs and functions are core competencies that must be handled and managed internally and which functions should be outsourced. Finally, we are implementing process changes that will enable us to operate more efficiently.

Q: What does "delayering" mean?

A: It means eliminating a layer or layers of management that create unnecessary bureaucracy, slow down decision making, and fail to add sufficient value to justify their cost. Updating the questions and answers will allow the employees to feel as if you are listening to them, and this will go a long way to build trust.

Another CMC intervention is the Pulse Survey. We talked about it earlier in the book, but now we will examine the advantages to conducting a survey focused solely on the restructuring effort. A Pulse Survey is *not* an employee engagement survey. When clients tell me that they just finished a voice of employee survey or engagement survey, my response every time is "They are not the same." The engagement survey focuses on retention and programs designed to make the company an employer of choice. The Pulse Survey is geared to understand how the organization feels regarding changes about to take place, senior leadership performance, and, most of all, their level of trust in the organization based on what they are hearing and seeing as a result of the restructuring. As in any change management endeavor, an emotional process takes place during restructuring. Understanding what the issues are will allow you to better communicate to given segments of the business. My firm's Pulse Survey is a customized program based on the company's organizational hierarchy, which breaks down the structure into easily identified regions, departments, and job titles for visibility into where the issues lie. This is important so that you can focus your efforts on the areas that need help. There are benchmarks for the survey, and we like to show a dashboard so clients can see the areas where improvement is required. A Pulse Survey and dashboard are shown in Exhibit 5.6.

The Communications Leader is the point person for the Pulse Survey. This person works with the leadership team to address the areas that are below benchmark, by incorporating an action plan that helps to remedy the low scores. These additional actions are added to the CMC strategy and tracked along with the rest of the change activities.

The survey is usually performed monthly or quarterly. I recommend monthly surveys. Since the organization is so integral to executing the restructuring changes, you have to be on top of areas of resistance or confusion, and remedy issues as soon as possible. If you don't focus on fixing the areas where there are issues, you will begin to see a decline in productivity and possibly involuntary attrition. It is not unusual to have low scores in the beginning, with a gradual increase as you begin deploying quick wins and the employees see progress. One significant piece of data that comes out of the Pulse Survey is how the organization feels about the SLT and the CEO. This is a powerful tool to use in performance management, along with other tools, such as the 360 assessment or

Company XYZ Enterprise	First Survey	Second Survey	Survey Average
Overall Score (1 = poor, 5 = excellent)	3.9	3.9	3.9
I am personally motivated to help Company XYZ succeed	4.4	4.3	4.4
I believe Company XYZ is headed in the right direction	3.6	3.7	3.6
I have no plans to leave Company XYZ within the next six months	4.2	4.1	4.1
I know how my job contributes to the success of our business	4.6	4.5	4.5
I thinkthe initiative will result in changes that will benefit my business unit	3.6	3.6	3.6
I understand why Company XYZ needs to make changes	4.2	4.2	4.2
I would recommend Company XYZ to a friend as a good place to work	3.7	3.6	3.7
My manager listens and responds to my feedback and concerns about our business/function	3.9	3.9	3.9
Company XYZ customers will benefit from the changes the company is making	3.6	3.6	3.6
Company XYZ gives me the opportunity to learn new skills and develop my career	3.7	3.7	3.7
Company XYZ senior management is focused on the long-term success of the company	3.8	3.8	3.8
The changes Company XYZ is making will create a better workplace	3.5	3.5	3.5
Have you been informed about the initiative?	4.7	4.8	4.7
Completed survey entries	6943	3686	10629

Exhibit 5.6 Pulse Survey

skip-level meeting. A 360 assessment is self-explanatory, but a skip level is not always understood.

In a skip-level meeting, managers meet with employees one level down to hear what is going on in their organization. The CEO and SLT should do these every two years, with action plans agreed to in order to tackle the issues that the manager isn't fixing. In some cases, you will gain a different view of how the manager performs from the meeting output, and you may need to take corrective action against the SLT member or manager. A Keirsey Assessment also adds to the equation and helps you understand if the innate skills of Senior Leadership Team members or managers' skills predisposed them to do their job well or not. We talk more about Keirsey in Chapter 7.

Changing an organization is probably one of the hardest things to do. You have to work diligently and consistently to change an organization successfully. If you have a solid CMC plan and build the proper foundation, implementing change will be much easier, and you'll improve the chances of success. If you're too impatient, or if you expect too many results too soon, your plans for change are more likely to fail, and you will lose the trust of the organization. Be mindful of these potential problems when you launch the individual workstreams, and try to create an environment where the restructuring is understood and supported.

Now that the project is kicked off and you understand the importance of your change management and communication plans, it is time to look at how to execute the activities in the framework that will deliver reduced cost and increased profit.

Notes

1. Dorothy Wardale, "Resource Kit: Rural Health Service Development: 4 Components of the Module," 2003.
2. John P. Kotter, "Winning at Change," *Leader to Leader* 10 (Fall 1998): 27–33.

Chapter 6

Executing the Framework

Moving from Conscious Incompetence to Conscious Competence

Congratulations! You have launched your restructuring project. It should be a relief that you have begun your initiative and prepared the organization for the changes about to occur. Knowing the positive benefits of this effort and the approach and tools you will use brings you further down the "Consciousness/Unconsciousness" Continuum. Now you know *what* the issues are and *how* you will fix them. You have it all figured out. It is time to put your plan into action and begin executing the multiple workstreams.

Organizational Efficiency

Let's start with Organizational Efficiency (OE) which we defined in Chapter 2, as the workstream that delivers short- and midterm improvements and cost savings. This workstream allows us to build an organizational structure that is "right sized" and flexible. We already have the organizational diagnostic assessment (ODA) results, so we know how good or bad the company structure is based on benchmarks. Now the goal is to prioritize the areas with the most opportunities and build a Work-Out calendar. We define what a Work-Out (WO!) is below, but how do you conduct one? Exhibit 6.1 outlines the standard steps to facilitate a WO!

When we talk about a Work-Out, people always look at me and say, "You mean workshop." And I say no, that's what consulting firms do. A WO! is something completely different, and not many people know how to facilitate one.

Jack Welch, the legendary GE CEO, first devised the concept of Work-Out as a way to reduce bureaucracy and give every employee, from managers to factory workers, an opportunity to influence and improve GE's day-to-day operations. Ultimately, the goal of Welch's Work-Out program was to clean up GE, to make

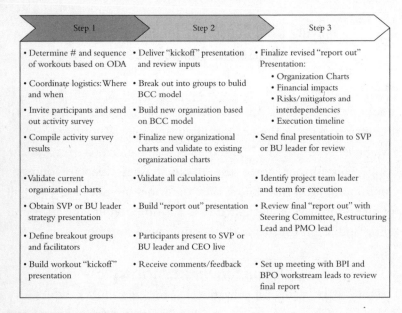

Step 1	Step 2	Step 3
• Determine # and sequence of workouts based on ODA	• Deliver "kickoff" presentation and review inputs	• Finalize revised "report out" Presentation:

• Coordinate logistics: Where and when	• Break out into groups to bulid BCC model	• Organization Charts
		  • Financial impacts
		  • Risks/mitigators and
		    interdependencies
		  • Execution timeline

• Invite participants and send out activity survey	• Build new organization based on BCC model	
• Compile activity survey results	• Finalize new organizational charts and validate to existing organizational charts	• Send final presentatioin to SVP or BU leader for review
• Validate current organizational charts	• Validate all calculatioins	• Identify project team leader and team for execution
• Obtain SVP or BU leader strategy presentation	• Build "report out" presentation	• Review final "report out" with Steering Committee, Restructuring Lead and PMO lead
• Define breakout groups and facilitators	• Participants present to SVP or BU leader and CEO live	
• Build workout "kickoff" presentation	• Receive comments/feedback	• Set up meeting with BPI and BPO workstream leads to review final report

Exhibit 6.1   OE Work-Out Process

workers more productive and processes simpler and more clear-cut. The program also was designed to reduce, and ultimately eliminate, all the wasted hours and energy that organizations like GE typically expend in performing day-to-day operations.[1]

How does it work? In Jack Welch's 2005 book, *Winning*, Work-Out is described as "groups of 30-100 employees would come together with an outside facilitator to discuss better ways of doing things and how to eliminate some of the beauracracy and roadblocks that were hindering them. The boss would be present at the beginning of each session, laying out the rationale for the Work-Out. He or she would also commit to two things: to give an on-the-spot yes or no to 75% of the recommendations that came out of the session, and to resolve the remaining 25% within 30 days."[2]

"I believe Work-Out was responsible for one of the most profound changes in GE during my time there. For the vast majority of employees, the boss-knows-all culture disappeared."

Although GE developed the WO! concept—and I learned the methodology there—I have redefined it dramatically for my firm as a process and tool for organizational redesign and work elimination. It is a progressive and innovative process, and we are the only firm in the world that uses this approach for organizational design. The key to WO! success is in knowing how to facilitate the process for the ultimate speed and results. A WO! is a fast-paced, collaborative session using multiple inputs and participants to design an optimal organization, and can last 48 to 72 hours, depending on the function or business being addressed. The process is rigorous, and participants and facilitators are lucky to finish before midnight each day. Most times the sessions go into the wee hours, with my team staying up all night to get the data and charts ready for the next day. Interestingly enough, we have never heard complaints from participants on how many hours they spend in the WO!, because they are so engaged and empowered by the process. I'm reminded of a funny story that took place while conducting a WO! with a client. I had a new senior consultant shadowing the process to learn how to conduct one. By the second day, the consultant, who was from an Ivy League school and worked at a well-respected best-in-class corporation, looked at me and said, "This is the hardest thing I have ever had to do. I can't believe the amount of work that goes into it and how much energy and information is shared during the session. The facilitator has to be great to pull this off."

Quick Tip

☞ Get your Organizational Development team trained in facilitation and Keirsey skills as soon as possible to lead the WO! or have people who are master facilitators trained in WO! before you officially launch the restructuring project. These skills will be valuable to the individual and to the company long term.

The Organizational Efficiency (OE) workstream is responsible for financial opportunities throughout the restructuring project, but it is the only workstream that delivers short-term financial benefits. OE is an iterative process because the organization's structure is constantly being redesigned based on the outputs from the Business Process Outsourcing (BPO) and Business Process Improvement (BPI) workstreams. As stated in Chapter 4, an organizational diagnostic assessment (ODA) should be performed every year to help realign resources based on the strategy road map and the changing business model. We use WO! as the tool to "right size" the organization and build the most optimal organization structure based on the ODA and other inputs. WO! also is a powerful change management tool, because you are building from the ground up using the experts in a department or business to define the roles and responsibilities, then develop the design of the organization. They know the work that is core and valuable and must be performed as well as the work that is noncore and does not add value to the business.

The first step to prepare the WO! participants to make the right decisions using facts, data, and analysis, along with their expert knowledge, is to complete the prework. Five inputs must be delivered to the WO! team before they can build the optimal organization structure.

1. Strategy road map and balanced scorecard
2. Organizational diagnostic assessment
3. Analysis of interviews
4. Current organizational charts, headcount, and payroll dollars
5. Activity survey

The inputs are collected by the OE workstream team and put into a document to be shared at the beginning of the WO!. The document acts as an educational tool, helping set the tone and point out issues within a function or business. It also outlines the issues and problems needing solving.

The first input for every Work-Out is the strategy road map and balanced scorecard. Additionally the function or business unit that is conducting the Work-Out supplies their strategy, which should be linked to the overall corporate strategy road map and scorecard pages with the function or business you are conducting the WO! for. This piece is developed and contributed to the Work-Out team by the SVP or business unit leader. By forcing the SVP or business leader to deliver his or her strategy to the Work-Out team, and have it directly linked to the master business strategy, we are creating the alignment that is so critical to the restructuring project.

The second input is the ODA, shown in Exhibit 6.2. The key here is to understand what this analysis is telling you. It should point to the opportunities immediately, conveying where there may be inefficiencies with the organization structure. When you understand the ODA, you can prioritize which functions or business units need to have Work-Outs performed first.

The third input is the interviews conducted by the OE workstream team. Here they are analyzed to identify trends, whether

Span of Control per Reporting Layer

Quick Facts:
- Compared to Professional Benchmark, Finance Worldwide has a 67.4% Span of Control Improvement Opportunity.
- Short Term = $2.2M • MidTerm $4.4M • Long Term $8.8M

Span of Control Improvement Opportunity is calculated based on # ppl mgrs and span of control gap

Reporting Layer	1	2	3	4	5	6	7	8	9	10
Finance Worldwide					5.2	5.8	4.8	4.7	8.0	
Finance Japan					7.0	5.8	4.6	5.8	-	-
Professional Benchmark					5.5	9.8	18.1	-	-	

Incumbents per Reporting Layer

Quick Facts:

Reporting Layers	Finance Worldwide 10	Finance Japan 10
Employees	1214	206
People Managers	224	36
Estimated payroll for Selection	$44M	$13M
Percentage group vs total data set	9.2%	1.6%

Reporting Layer	1	2	3	4	5	6	7	8	9	10	11
Finance Worldwide	0	0	0	0	5	30	153	408	431	187	0
Finance Japan	0	0	0	0	2	7	42	67	80	8	0

Distribution by Reporting Level

Quick Facts:
- Finance Worldwide: 0% of the population is in reporting layers 1–3
- Finance Worldwide: 2.9% of the population is in reporting layers 4–6
- Finance Worldwide: 97.1% of the population is in reporting layers 7 and up

- Finance Japan: 0% of the population is in reporting layers 1–3
- Finance Japan: 4.4% of the population is in reporting layers 4–6
- Finance Japan: 95.6% of the population is in reporting layers 7 and up

Reporting Layer	1	2	3	4	5	6	7	8	9	10	11
Finance Worldwide	0.00%	0.00%	0.00%	0.00%	0.41%	2.47%	12.60%	33.61%	35.50%	15.40%	0.00%
Finance Japan	0.00%	0.00%	0.00%	0.00%	0.97%	3.40%	20.39%	32.52%	38.83%	3.88%	0.00%

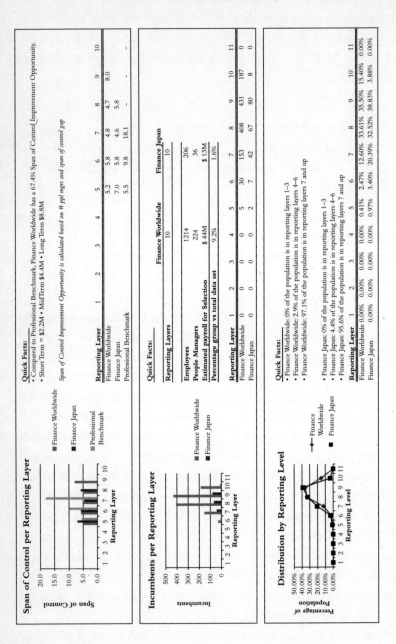

Exhibit 6.2 Organizational Diagnostic Assessment

areas that need improvement or changes already in play. The interviews are eye openers. Completing the interviews is only the first step. The OE workstream must also perform analysis on the information you receive. My firm likes to use Pareto charts (Exhibits 6.3 and 6.4) and fishbone diagrams (Exhibit 6.5), which are Six Sigma tools, but you can use any analysis tools you like. In the examples in these exhibits, we highlight the issues with compensation for a global sales organization.

The next input is the current organizational charts, along with number of full-time equivalents (FTEs) and payroll data. These are used in conjunction with the ODA to better understand the roles in the layers. The FTE and payroll numbers are important; you will need to do a variance report indicating the delta in the number of heads and costs for the new organization. Your financial opportunities calculations are derived from this step.

The final input is the Activity Survey, which is critical to understanding how the function or business is spending its time. My firm has a program that identifies all the activities and tasks a function or business performs, then has the people who execute those activities indicate how much time they spend on them during the course of a normal day. It always amazes me how much time employees are spending on non–value-added administrative and transactional work. I wonder: Are the managers creating this non–value-added work, or are the employees producing the work to stay busy? Probably a little of both. In any event, the work needs to be rated, and the result will be something like the visual in Exhibit 6.6. In order to gather all the data, you will need approximately four weeks before the actual Work-Out.

Now that you have all the inputs, the workstream team needs to synthesize it and create the story that will be communicated on the first day of the Work-Out. Key points of the story should be what the data shows, and all the backup data should be made available for WO! participants to view.

The inputs are only one dimension of the Work-Out; the participants make up the other dimension. Our OE and BPI

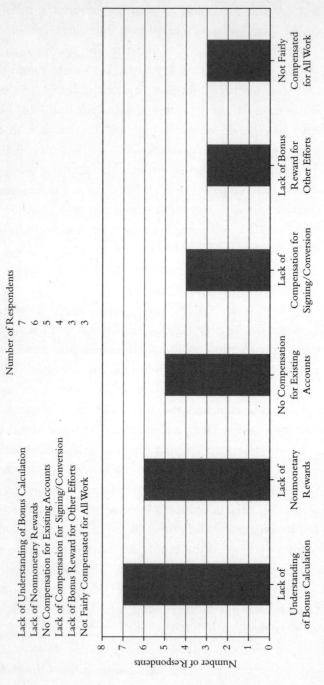

	Number of Respondents
Lack of Understanding of Bonus Calculation	7
Lack of Nonmonetary Rewards	6
No Compensation for Existing Accounts	5
Lack of Compensation for Signing/Conversion	4
Lack of Bonus Reward for Other Efforts	3
Not Fairly Compensated for All Work	3

Exhibit 6.3 U.S. Focus Group—People Issues

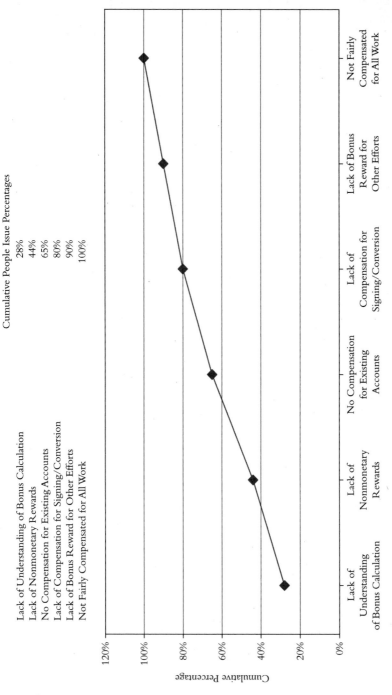

Cumulative People Issue Percentages

Lack of Understanding of Bonus Calculation   28%
Lack of Nonmonetary Rewards   44%
No Compensation for Existing Accounts   65%
Lack of Compensation for Signing/Conversion   80%
Lack of Bonus Reward for Other Efforts   90%
Not Fairly Compensated for All Work   100%

Exhibit 6.4 U.S. Focus Group—Cumulative People Issues Percentages

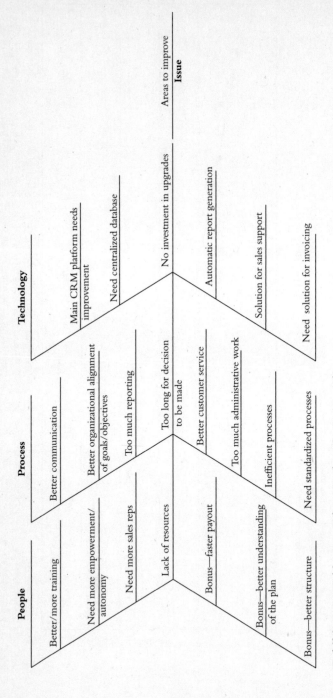

Exhibit 6.5 Fishbone—What Needs to Be Improved?

People
- Better/more training
- Need more empowerment/autonomy
- Need more sales reps
- Lack of resources
- Bonus—faster payout
- Bonus—better understanding of the plan
- Bonus—better structure

Process
- Better communication
- Better organizational alignment of goals/objectives
- Too much reporting
- Too long for decision to be made
- Better customer service
- Too much administrative work
- Inefficient processes
- Need standardized processes

Technology
- Main CRM platform needs improvement
- Need centralized database
- No investment in upgrades
- Automatic report generation
- Solution for sales support
- Need solution for invoicing

Issue
- Areas to improve

Sample Enterprise XYZ Results, *June 2008*

XYZ Enterprise Overall Score (1 = Poor, 5 = Excellent)	Week 7/21	Week 7/14	Week 7/7	Grand Average
I am satisfied with information I am receiving on XYZ's project.	4.0	3.9	3.9	3.9
I am personally motivated to help XYZ succeed.	3.6	3.5	3.5	3.5
I know how my job contributes to the success of our business.	3.4	3.4	3.3	3.3
XYZ offers me the opportunity to learn new skills and develop my career.	3.6	3.6	3.5	3.6
I am accountable for my results.	3.8	3.5	3.5	3.5
My manager listens and responds to my feedback and concerns about our business/function.	3.5	3.4	3.3	3.3
I feel adequately recognized when I do a good job.	3.3	3.1	3.1	3.1
I have no plans to leave XYZ within the next six months.	3.5	3.5	3.4	3.4
I understand XYZ's vision and strategy for the future.	3.3	3.3	3.3	3.3
I am confident in the leadership of XYZ's senior management.	4.2	4.1	4.0	4.0
I would recommend XYZ to a friend as a good place to work.	4.3	4.2	4.1	4.2
XYZ customers will benefit from the changes the company is making.	3.4	3.5	3.3	3.3
Company policies and procedures are applied consistently across my department.	4.3	4.2	4.2	4.2
I believe XYZ will reinvest some of the project savings back into the company.	3.9	3.8	3.7	3.7
XYZ is becoming more customer focused.	3.4	3.4	3.3	3.3
	4.0	4.0	3.9	3.9
Completed Survey Entries	52	468	5058	5578

Can sort by:

> Function Unit (Human Resources, Finance, . . .)
> Company position (individual contributor, manager, director, executive)
> Tenure (less than 1 year, 1–3 years . . .)
> Country (United States, UK)

Legend

4.25–5.00	Green
3.75–4.25	Yellow
0.00–3.75	Red

Exhibit 6.6 Pulse Survey

processes require working with layers below the vice president, typically layers 4 and 5. These are the people actually "doing the work" rather than managing. They are also the subject matter experts and technical experts. They know where the issues are and can help define what needs to be done to fix them. If you are a global company, you should invite people from each region, for a total of about 20 to 24 people, and distribute a very loose agenda. Because this process is all about innovation and inspiration, holding the group to a rigid schedule is not appropriate. The facilitator is important here. He or she must gauge the group's progress and know when to push group members and when to let them argue it out . . . and they will argue!

Quick Tip

☞ A Work-Out is intense. Emotions fly due to the sensitive nature of what's being discussed and the participants' lack of sleep. In some cases, the results will lead to eliminating a friend's job, their boss' job, or even their own. To limit the sensitivity, we recommend *not* listing people's names on organizational charts, just titles.

The next step in the process is the actual Work-Out. I developed the WO! to follow the Forming—Storming—Norming—Performing model of group development was first proposed by Bruce Tuckman in 1965. He maintained that these phases are all necessary and inevitable in order for the team to grow, face up to challenges, tackle problems, find solutions, plan work, and deliver results. If you have ever worked in an intense collaborative team environment, you have been through these steps and may not have known it.

We begin with the kickoff presentation that includes the strategy road map, balanced scorecard, the SVP or Business Unit

100

(BU) leader's strategy, and all the prework analysis. The SVP or BU leader is the presenter and must demonstrate his or her alignment with the restructuring project. This person should be a positive change advocate and give the team the freedom to build whatever they think is the best structure to deliver on the strategy. After the SVP or BU leader delivers the presentation, he or she leaves until the last day, when the Work-Out team presents its recommendations. Many participants initially feel scared or threatened, and they will call or get calls from their manager wanting to know what is going on. But rule number one is: What happens in the Work-Out stays in the Work-Out! Leaking information is dangerous to business productivity. Until the CEO signs off on the recommendations, nothing gets communicated.

Now that the context has been established, the WO! team divides into groups to complete the Business Core Competency Model (BCCM). They rate the activities from the activity survey, using two axes. One axis is based on performance (how well the company does it) and maturity (how mature the process is (i.e., automated or manual), while the other axis is how strategic the activity is to the business. Based on the ratings, the activities are plotted. The end result looks something like what you see in Exhibit 6.7.

The activities fall into one of three sections:

1. **Core.** Delivers a competitive advantage to generate revenue and profit to the business (i.e., sales).
2. **Center of Expertise (COE).** Expertise that enables the competitive advantage work to occur (i.e., recruiting).
3. **Shared Service**. Necessary work that must be performed but is not a competitive advantage or enabler to the business (i.e., benefits administration).

Once the breakout groups have completed the BCCM, the groups join together to review and discuss the assessments. This can be a very long session, which each participant having his or her own

Function: Business Operations

Main Category	Process Maturity	Strategic Value
(1) 1.1 Define the business concept and long-term vision	2.00	6.33
(2) 1.2 Develop business strategy	2.00	7.00
(3) 2.1 Manage product and service portfolio	2.95	7.43
(4) 3.2 Develop marketing strategy	2.00	6.50
(5) 3.3 Develop sales strategy	2.00	7.00
(6) 3.4 Develop and manage marketing plans	2.00	8.00
(7) 3.5 Develop and manage sales plans	3.00	6.50
(8) 4.2 Procure materials and services	3.36	3.47
(9) 4.4 Deliver service to customer	3.74	3.80
(10) 4.5 Manage logistics and warehousing	4.87	4.03
(11) 7.4 Manage enterprise information	4.00	7.00
(12) 8.2 Perform revenue accounting	4.00	4.00
(13) 8.6 Process accounts payable and expense reimbursements	4.00	5.50
(14) 8.8 Manage internal controls	3.00	4.50

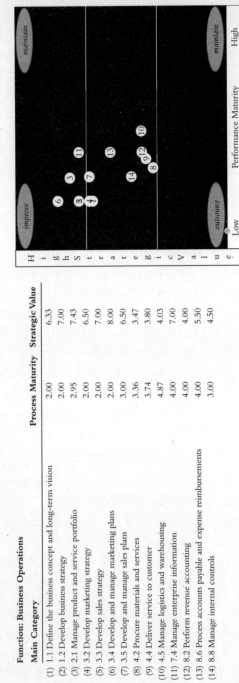

Exhibit 6.7 Business Core Competency Model

opinion of where the activities fall. But the facilitator must remind them of how the ratings are determined and why, and push the group to come to alignment . . . not concensus trying to achieve that at this time will not get you anywhere. The meeting can get pretty ugly.

Now that the groups have agreed on what activities are plotted in core, COE, and shared services, you can begin to build the organization structure. The breakout groups go back and begin to look for synergies where they can consolidate roles and gain economies of scale by merging functions that have similar activities. They also look at how to build COEs, which are generally small in nature, and shared services, which are either insourced or outsourced and consist of large numbers of employees.

COEs have been around for years, but most companies don't build them correctly. They are small areas of expertise with employees who are responsible for developing standard processes and tools to be rolled out to the function or BU to be implemented. *COEs do not implement!* They are a handful of people at most, and usually virtual. The old days of housing everyone together is gone. With technology, there is no reason you can't have COE leaders in different countries or states. They can be regional as well, especially if certain regulations pertain to your work in one part of the world but are not applicable elsewhere.

Shared services also often are built incorrectly. Most people think of outsourcing when they hear the term "shared services." Although outsourcing is a very cost-effective way to manage necessary transactional work, shared services can be in house as well. Again, they don't need to be sitting all together; rather, they need access to the right technology and standard processes and templates to perform their jobs consistently across the enterprise.

My firm likes to bring best-in-class organizational structures into the Work-Out to help the participants think innovatively about how the work activities can get done. If you can purchase some through benchmarking companies, it is a great input into the design process.

As the breakout groups are building the organizational structures, they must be reminded that this is future state. They must understand that things will need to occur in order for the new design to be implemented.

After the breakout groups design their organizational structure, they are again brought together for review and discussion. This is where the arguing can get pretty bad, but it's all part of the process, and again the facilitator must be strong. This design process continues several times until the breakout groups feel they have achieved the goals the SVP or BU leader identified in the strategy and that they have addressed all the inputs given to them in the kickoff presentation. The new organizational structure may have all three elements or two or just one. It must, however, contain the correct number of layers and spans of control based on the ODA benchmark. An example is detailed in Exhibit 6.8.

Once the breakout groups agree on the structures, it's time to work on the risks, mitigants and interdependencies, using the templates from Chapter 3. The goal for the group is to identify the

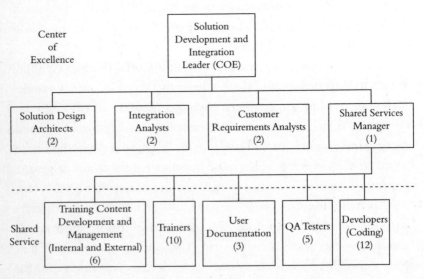

Exhibit 6.8   OE Organizational Design Example

risks to implementing this structure and how to mitigate them. The group must also identify the interdependencies, including work that must be performed by the other workstreams in order for the structure to be optimal. An example of a risk might be resistance from customers to accept the new model. The mitigating factor might be to hold customer education sessions to review the benefits of the new model. Independencies are very important, because they usually are the roadblocks to implementing a new structure immediately. An example might be: Technology platform needs to be upgraded to automate manual processes. This is not just an output for IT but also for the Business Process Improvement workstream, which will need to reengineer the process from manual to automated.

Now that you have the organizational structure, risks, mitigants and interdependencies, it's time to develop the new roles that will be in the organization. This is important to do during the Work-Out stage so team members can provide input on competencies and/or skills that currently are missing from the function or BU.

By now you have become a collaborative team and are ready to present your recommendations to the SVP or BU leader and the CEO. The process works best if the CEO is present, because it limits the SVP's or BU leader's ability to augment the recommendations dramatically before the CEO sees them. The CEO may have a different point of view from the SVP and BU leader, and this gives him or her the chance to give direct feedback to the team and the SVP or BU leader immediately. It also helps move things along quickly. If you wait for the SVP or BU leader to meet with the CEO for his or her approval, it could be weeks or months before you get the approval to move forward. Each breakout group assigns presenters responsible for reviewing the recommendations to the SVP /BU leader and CEO presenting him or her breakout group's so it is very important that the entire team stands behind the recommendations and that there are not people who are against the recommendation at the point.

At this point, you have received feedback, and the team is ready to revise their recommendations and go home. I will tell you, if conducted correctly, this process will change the participants' work life. They will become change advocates and also will have learned how to build an optimal organization. One comment from a participant I remember in particular: "That was wild: I can't believe how much we got accomplished in three days! It would have taken my business six or nine months to do this, and I am not sure it would come out the way our recommendations did."

As the Work-Out team was designing the organizational structure, you should have identified a Project Team Leader to manage the transition to the new organization. This person will also work with the BPI and business BPO workstreams to share the outcomes and identify opportunities. The person also works with finance to validate the financial opportunities identified in the Work-Out and to track, along with the financial analyst in the PMO) the realization of those opportunities.

The Project Team Leader is a full-time role that lasts until the restructuring project is complete. Due to the amount of iterations the organization will take on, it is important for one person to own the changes and manage the communication along with the Change Management and Communications Leader. The Project Team Leader reports into the PMO and may have responsibility for all the organization changes or just one function or business unit. Regardless, you must have a very strong project manager who can work with human resources, finance, IT, legal, and other areas to accomplish all the tasks that go into a organization restructuring.

You have finished your Work-Outs and captured short-term benefits for the business. Now what? You must be patient. You must wait for the BPO and BPI worksteams to deliver their opportunities. Because the OE workstream is dependent on these workstreams for additional benefits, a regular schedule and reports are necessary to keep the OE workstream leader informed of what is coming down the pike for possible changes to the organization structure.

The case study in Exhibit 6.9 represents a global consumer services company that we worked with recently. As you can see, the company learned all the proper OD practices and implemented a great sales organization. As of this book going to press, only four months after the implementation, the company was already seeing the benefits in revenue growth.

Exhibit 6.9   Global Sales OE Work-Out Case Study

Company

$6B Global Consumer Services Company

Challenge

The global sales organization was siloed and, although global, each region worked autonomously, without leveraging standard processes, knowledge-sharing or cross-selling opportunities across the company. Additionally, the lack of streamlined, efficient processes led to a significant administrative burden to the sales force, preventing salespeople from spending time on the street selling and generating revenue.

Approach

NexGen's approach consisted of structuring a plan using several tools and processes to identify issues, root causes. The plan included:

1. Performing an organizational diagnostic assessment of the structure's layers and spans of control
2. Process mapping to identify inefficient processes and then reengineer
3. Interviews resulting in building fishbones and Paretos to highlight the issues needing to be addressed
4. Conducting a three-day Work-Out using all the above inputs to design the optimal organization

The three-day global sales Work-Out attended by a select group of 24 sales professionals resulted in a redesigned, truly global organization rectifying all the challenges that had been identified as well as achieving the goals the SVP of sales had communicated in the beginning of the session.

Results

NexGen advisors restructured the global sales organization into a more efficient structure by developing centers of excellence to create standard

---

enterprise-wide processes and centralized subject matter experts for easier access to information. Additionally, we created administrative hubs to manage the non value-added transactional support in a more efficient and cost-effective manner.

For the global sales organization, this meant that the administrative burden was decreased significantly, allowing for more time with customers; the structure was optimized for cross-selling opportunities, leading to increased revenue opportunities; and the sales organization was globally integrated with fewer layers for more empowerment and to support the global customer base more effectively.

The end state result was a better leverage of the existing sales force in the field driving toward significantly higher productivity and revenue growth.

Exhibit 6.9 (*Continued*)

Now let us review the mid- and long-term opportunities: BPI and BPO.

Business Process Improvement

We begin our Business Process Improvement (BPI) effort simultaneously, using output from our OE sessions as inputs into our BPI workstream and processes. When you think about BPI, what comes to mind? Lean, Six Sigma, Total Quality Management (TQM), Kaizen. You may have some familiarity with these methodologies, but how do you use them in a restructuring environment? You would execute them as you would execute them in a regular business environment, but faster. This section of the book describes how to set up your teams and execute the BPI process using various quality tools. It is not a course on how to use the tools. For that, you will need to study the specific methodology you want to use. This text uses examples to take you through the steps necessary to execute BPI for a particular process in your

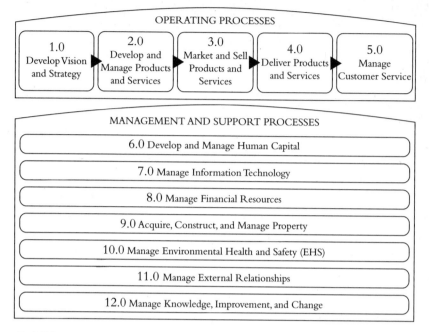

Exhibit 6.10 APQC Process Classification Framework[SM] Level 1 Categories

company, describe what the output from a working session should look like, and provide a case study for your reference.

As we discussed in Chapter 4, understanding the state of your business is the first step in knowing where to start your BPI effort. Out of all the areas in the self-assessment, which ones have you repeatedly had the most problems with based on feedback from customers, warranty/repair reports, and customer service calls? Make sure you are not just looking at where the issues show up; also consider what upstream problems could be driving the negative outcomes. Typically we use the American Productivity and Quality Center (APQC) Process Classification Framework[SM] (PCF) shown in Exhibit 6.10, to break down the siloed organizations of a company into categories and operating processes.

For example, a Product Development organization is actually part of the overall APQC category 2.0—Develop and Manage Products and Services. The framework defines where the beginning and end of every process should occur in a typical organization. There are benchmarks for each process, so you can perform apples-to-apples comparisons against other companies in your industry or all companies that have provided data to APQC. These processes may overlap with those of other organizations in your company, depending on the structure and responsibilities you have defined for your specific organization. Knowing where the responsibilities of your organization begin and end is important in order for you to include the right team members on the projects and implement the correct metrics to track improvements during and after the project. You can focus your effort on only the processes that repeatedly have issues, but we recommend performing BPI on all processes in your company, even if you do so in a phased approach. Exhibit 6.11 is the process you will follow for each of the APQC Level 1 categories that you want to improve.

The first thing you do before starting your effort is to create your team by assigning leaders to APQC categories even if the categories are not going to be looked at until later in the project. These people, called Continuous Improvement (CI) Champions, will be responsible and accountable for everything that happens in their category. They should be Six Sigma trained, at a minimum. These people report to the Restructuring Lead and form a BPI committee that meets weekly to review progress in their areas and share best practices. The document used to review projects can be defined by the BPI committee, but make sure the elements that make up the template include the elements that will be reviewed on the status template by the Steering Committee.

In our example, this individual would lead all the efforts related to Product Development or the APQC category 2.0—Develop and Manage Products and Services.

Product Development Example

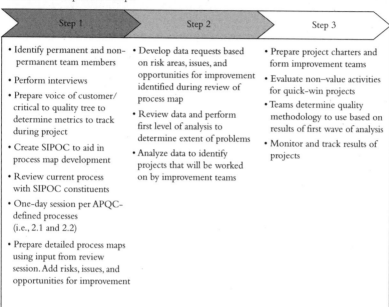

Step 1	Step 2	Step 3
• Identify permanent and non-permanent team members	• Develop data requests based on risk areas, issues, and opportunities for improvement identified during review of process map	• Prepare project charters and form improvement teams
• Perform interviews		• Evaluate non–value activities for quick-win projects
• Prepare voice of customer/critical to quality tree to determine metrics to track during project	• Review data and perform first level of analysis to determine extent of problems	• Teams determine quality methodology to use based on results of first wave of analysis
• Create SIPOC to aid in process map development	• Analyze data to identify projects that will be worked on by improvement teams	• Monitor and track results of projects
• Review current process with SIPOC constituents		
• One-day session per APQC-defined processes (i.e., 2.1 and 2.2)		
• Prepare detailed process maps using input from review session. Add risks, issues, and opportunities for improvement		

Exhibit 6.11   BPI Process

Quick Tip

☞ Leaders for these categories must be strong, proven, and respected. They do not have to be from the organization they are leading. As a matter of fact, it is often better to have someone from outside the organization, so only data-driven improvements are implemented. People within the organization tend to discount suggestions very easily, saying "We already tried that and it didn't work" or "We don't need data, I know the problem is _____." Intuition can be deadly to true process improvement.

Once a CI Champion is chosen for the category and you have chosen which process to focus on first, you are now ready to fill the

Process Owner and Program Manager positions that make up the Level 2 processes of the APQC Process Classification Framework^{SM} in Exhibit 6.12. In the case of our product development example, two distinct Level 2 processes, 2.1 Manage product and service portfolio and 2.2 Develop products and services, roll up to the category 2.0 Develop and Manage Products and Services. Process owners are the operating personnel who are responsible for the day-to-day activities of the Level 2 processes, typically at the general manager (GM) level. They serve mainly as advisors but they are also there to remove roadblocks that may hinder a team. If there are several GMs with responsibility in a category, pick the ones who have the most responsibility in the Level 2 processes.

The next positions to fill are those of the Program Managers. They are the team leaders for each of the Level 2 processes and report to the CI Champion of the category. They should come from the organization they work in but not necessarily from the Level 2 process they will lead. Exhibit 6.13 depicts what a typical BPI structure for our product development example looks like.

Quick Tip

☞ Program Managers leading Level 2 processes should be Six Sigma Black Belt certified. If they are not certified, at a minimum they should attend Black Belt or Green Belt training.

Now that the key leaders running the BPI effort have been identified, identical paths are taken to execute. Each Program Manager must determine and then get approval from the operations leader responsible for that category, where the responsibility for their process starts and stops. In the case of our example, the SVP of product development needs to agree that processes 2.1 and 2.2 start and stop where the Program Manager suggests, even

Level 1 = Category	Level 2 = Process	Level 3 = Process
1 Develop Vision and Strategy		
	1.1 Define the business concept and long-term vision	
	1.2 Develop business strategy	
	1.3 Manage strategic initiatives	
2 Develop and Manage Products and Services		
	2.1 Manage product and service portfolio	
		2.1.1 Evaluate performance of existing products/services against market opportunities
		2.1.2 Define product/service development requirements
		2.1.3 Perform discovery research
		2.1.4 Confirm alignment of product/service concepts with business strategy
		2.1.5 Manage product and service life cycle
	2.2 Develop products and services	
		2.2.1 Design, build, and evaluate products and services
		2.2.2 Test market for new or revised products and services
		2.2.3 Prepare for production
3 Market and Sell Products and Services		
	3.1 Understand markets, customers, and capabilities	
	3.2 Develop marketing strategy	
	3.3 Develop sales strategy	
	3.4 Develop and manage marketing plans	
	3.5 Develop and manage sales plans	

Exhibit 6.12 APQC Process Classification Framework[SM] Level 1, Subprocesses 2–3

113

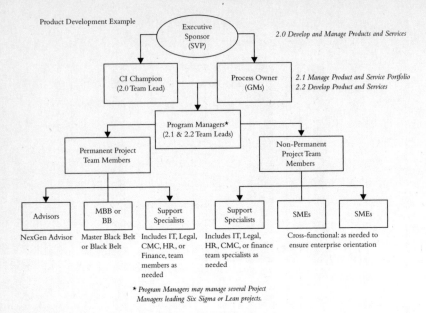

Exhibit 6.13 Typical BPI Team Structure

if those processes are outside the boundaries of his or her current organization. The SVP must get approval from the leader running any overlapping processes. For this reason, communication and cooperation among everyone involved is critical to ensure that changes are not being made without input and agreement from all leaders who have a stake in the process.

The APQC Process Classification Framework[SM] is helpful because it details the subprocesses to Level 4, which makes it easy to see where processes start and stop. It is important to try to use the APQC taxonomy when structuring your organizations; most companies are organized in this way, making it easy to benchmark themselves against other companies. If you want to measure yourself against a benchmark, you need to have processes that are standard across companies worldwide.

Now that the boundaries for each Level 2 process have been determined, you are ready to begin in-depth interviews of key personnel who are part of the process: a process customer, or a process supplier. Interviews are important because standard questions are used to get input, and issues or comments that are repeated can be monitored.

Interviews are also helpful when determining which resources should be on your team. It is best to have team members who are internal to the organization being improved or who are customers and suppliers to your organization. An upstream supplier of product development, for example, is sales and marketing. Sales and marketing need to supply product development with their specific needs and requirements for your processes to run smoothly. By having the supplier who has input into your process on the team, understanding the issues and improvements to the process benefits the upstream processes as well. This approach of including suppliers and customers into the process redesign allows you to focus on your internal processes instead of worrying about or complaining about hand-offs from the upstream organization. Likewise, a supplier to downstream processes supply chain and manufacturing, you must understand their requirements so you can provide them with what they need, eliminating issues in their process that are not internally generated. Exhibit 6.14 lists 13 commonly asked interview questions. The answers generated from these interviews become the

---

1. In terms of your responsibility, what is the first activity performed?
2. In terms of your responsibility, what is the last activity performed?
3. At a high level, what are the key activities that are performed in your process?
4. What is the variation in the process for different products or service offerings?
5. What is the variation in the process for international versus domestic customers?
6. Who are the other employees that are involved in this process?
7. What activities do you think your organization does well?
8. What technology or tools do you have that enable you to perform those activities?
9. What activities does your organization not perform well?
10. Where do you have issues? What are the inputs to those issues? Who is the owner of those issues?
11. What technology or tools do you need to do those above-mentioned activities better?
12. If you could change how your organization performs activities, what would you change?
13. Do you have any metrics by which your process is measured?

Exhibit 6.14   Common Interview Questions

basis for the voice of the customer (VOC) sessions and are inputs during the development of a SIPOC (suppliers, inputs, process, outputs, and customers).

Quick Tip

☞ It is helpful to have one person ask the questions during the interview and another person take the notes.

After the interviews are completed, you probably will have a good sense of who should be on your project teams. Getting approval to use these people can sometimes be difficult, but if this effort is being championed by the CEO (which it should be), there should not be any pushback. Most team members are only part time, averaging roughly 20 percent of their work hours. Some members may have to spend more time on the project, especially those whose responsibilities or activities may change due to implementation of process improvements.

We are now ready to start using Six Sigma tools to help us with our BPI effort. The importance of customer involvement and feedback has been mentioned a few times. It is necessary to have your internal and external customers participate in VOC sessions so your organization's goals align with their needs. This session gets all the customers of a process together in one room to create a "critical to quality" (CTQ) tree. It lays out the customer needs from the process, the quality drivers that will allow customer needs to be met, and the CTQ characteristics that can be measured and monitored to show improvement. An example of the output from a VOC session, which is a CTQ tree, is depicted in Exhibit 6.15.

At the same time, you can create an APQC Level 3 subprocess SIPOC from your interview output and the input from your VOC session. The SIPOC may take several iterations because you need

Customer Needs	Quality Driver	CTQs
Service (software) offers sold globally	• Standardized offers released globally	% of service offers available in all countries % of service offers with standardized collateral
	• Training provided to sales associates	% of new offers for which training is provided % of sales organization receiving certification on new offers
	• Services offers easily ordered with product (hardware)	% of services sold with hardware versus plan Cycle time to configure and propose service offer
Offering performs within specifications	• Product failures tracked, managed, and recorded	# of warranty calls versus plan for all products % of product failures report % of incidents with costs recorded % of resolutions implemented % of EEs with metrics tied to product performance
	• Incident reduction actions supported by product development	% and # of incidents resolved by product development % of incidents with material changes made to offers % of incidents with additional training as cause

Exhibit 6.15 Voice of Customer to Critical to Quality Tree

all parties involved in the process need to review the SIPOC before you can move to the next step. SMEs should review the SIPOC, including customers, suppliers, and process experts, but not managers. If you involve managers only, you will not have the appropriate level of detail. Additional interviews with SMEs may be necessary to complete the SIPOC. Exhibit 6.16 offers an example of a SIPOC for the Level 2 process, 2.1 Manage product and service portfolio.

When you have completed your VOC session and received approval on your SIPOC, you can begin to process map your Level 3 APQC subprocesses. It is critical to perform the mapping at this level in order to identify root cause issues. If you map your processes at too high a level, you will fix symptoms, not root causes. This session takes a significant amount of planning because you want to make sure you have the right people and agenda that will allow you to get all the information you need. If you have several different product offerings (e.g., hardware, software, services) with global manufacturing locations, you need representation from all of them. You also need to map each of the individual processes if they differ from each other. Typically, this process mapping session lasts up to a week, with between 35 to 50 participants from all over the world. It includes internal customers and suppliers as well as the SMEs who were identified during the creation of the SIPOC. The session is a large expense but is well worth the effort.

Now let us look at how to perform the process mapping, the tool you need to capture the data during the session, and next steps after the session. From the process maps, projects will be identified by the CI Leader and put into the queue to be reviewed by the Steering Committee for prioritization and funding. The leader of the operation can also agree to fund the projects out of his or her own budget, but make sure the funding is tied to the restructuring project funding and savings template, so you can get a true picture of the effort, both savings and investment.

Manage Product and Service Portfolio

Suppliers:	Inputs:	Process	Outputs:	Customers:
Product Manager, Product Marketing, Industry Marketing, Sales-Solution/Product, Customers, Strategy and Planning	technology trends and road maps, market assessments, competitive assessment, strategic plan, customer requirements, customer requirements, specific solution ideas	2.1.1 Evaluate performance against market	high-level offer description, preliminary business impact model, potential business case, preliminary value proposition	Product Manager, Business Impact Modeling, Product Marketing, Industry Marketing, Service Design, Services Product Management
Product Manager, Business Impact Modeling, Product Marketing, Industry Marketing, Service Design, Service Product Management	high-level offer description, preliminary business impact model, potential business case, preliminary value proposition	2.1.2 Define development requirements	updated value proposition, updated business case/ROI, TCO plan, project plan, risks, preliminary product & service requirements, technology requirements, arch/design considerations	Industry Marketing, Product Marketing, Services Product Management, Service Design, Engineering Management, HW Architecture Design
Industry Marketing, Product Manager, Services Product Management, Service Design, Engineering Management, HW Architecture Design	updated value proposition, updated business case/ROI, TCO plan, project plan, risks, preliminary product & service requirements, technology requirements, arch/design considerations	2.1.3 Perform discovery research	final product/service requirements, solution architecture, technology partners, patent/IP strategy, functional specifications, high-level design, production sourcing plan, delivery/support plan, issue resolution plan, security plan	Product Manager, HW Architecture, Services Product Management, Service Design, Engineering Management, Commodity Management, Supply Chain Management, Quality, Sales-Solution/Product, Engineering Project Management
Product Manager, HW Architecture Design, Services Product Management, Service Design, Engineering Management, Commodity Management, Intellectual Property, Supply Chain Management, Quality, Engineering Project Management	final product/service requirements, solution architecture, technology partners, patent/IP strategy, functional specifications, high-level design, TCO pricing strategy, production sourcing plan, delivery/support plan, issue resolution plan, security plan	2.1.4 Confirm alignment of concepts with business strategy	validated design with accept testing, pricing strategy and price list, sales collateral, training materials, production sourcing plan, final deployment plan, service support plan, quality measurements	Product Manager, Industry Marketing, Services Product Management, Service Design, Engineering Management, Commodity Management, Supply Chain Management, Quality, Sales-Solution/Product, Services Program Management, Logistics
Product Manager, Industry Marketing, Services Product Management, Service Design, Engineering Management, Supply Chain Management, Quality, Sales-Solution/Product, PS Application Integration Serv (SSM), PS Program Management (SSM), Logistics (GCO-WCS)	validated design with accept testing, pricing strategy and price list, sales collateral, training materials, production sourcing plan, final deployment plan, service support plan, quality measurements	2.1.5 Manage product and service life cycle	end-to-end solution, control set results, corrective action plans, availability plans, final services support plan, customer requirements feedback mechanism, service production plan, field retrofit process plan, product phase in/phase out plan, product and service discontinuation plan	Product Manager, Industry Marketing, Services Product Management, Service Design, PS Business Consulting, Engineering Management, Commodity Management, Supply Chain Management, Quality, Manufacturing Engineering, Sales-Solution/Product, Services Application/Integration Service, Services Program Management, Logistics

Exhibit 6.16 SIPOC

119

Process mapping for BPI differs from traditional process mapping but uses the same symbols. The desired outcome of the process-mapping session is to have a complete map for each of the APQC Level 3 subprocesses that roll up to the Level 2 process. So, for example, using the product development example, the Level 2 process, 2.1 Manage product and services portfolio, would have five process maps that would roll up to it: processes 2.1.1, 2.1.2, 2.1.3, 2.1.4, and 2.1.5. The other Level 2 process within product development, 2.2 Develop product and services, will have three processes mapped: 2.2.1, 2.2.2, and 2.2.3. An example is shown in Exhibit 6.16.

Each step of the process is documented, noting the resource/ organization (e.g., software engineering) that is responsible for executing the task. You also specify whether the task has a high risk of failure. If it has a high risk associated with it or is a known issue, more information is captured. By "risk," we mean that if the task fails, there is a potential loss of revenue, rework, or a symptom shows up downstream. A high risk means that it either happens often or doesn't happen often but is a big issue when it does occur. Medium means it doesn't happen very often and is easily resolved. Low risk means the problem rarely occurs. Many of these risks will come from your customers downstream. Be realistic about risks because they will be what drive your improvement projects. You will capture the issue or risk, the field/metric for which you will gather data and perform analysis, and any actual metrics that SMEs or customer service personnel know or have. Refer to the example process map in Exhibit 6.17.

Capturing the data you get from the process-mapping session is an important task. Exhibit 6.18 presents the product development process and an example data capture template, showing the necessary fields. One person in the session should be responsible for and ensuring that owners are identified for each action item captured. This is also the person who will follow-up and track all actions. Most of the actions will involve getting data or reports from the

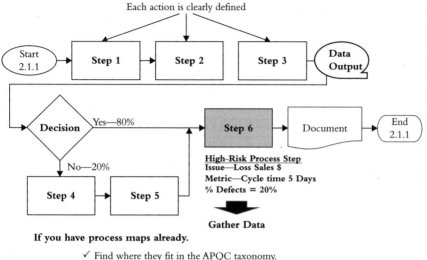

Exhibit 6.17   BPI Process Map

SMEs or customer service personnel so analysis can be performed to see the extent of the issue identified. For issues that do not have metrics, either programming is needed to retrieve the data from various systems in the company or manual data capture for a short period of time may be necessary. It is absolutely critical to ensure that the data is clean and valid. We recommend having an internal auditor resource dedicated to the project to audit the data files that are produced from data requests. You must follow a strict process for data requests and validation; otherwise, you will fix the wrong things. We recommend the process for data validation in Chapter 3.

Once you have the data files, the program managers or Master Black Belts/Black Belts who work for them can start using different analysis techniques to understand the severity and root causes of issues identified during the process mapping session. Take the time to do the analysis correctly so you can fix the root causes. Don't rush to judgment based on intuitive input from others. You have

Exhibit 6.18 Data Capture Template

Risk Area	Process	Issue	Risk or Impact	Impact Rating	Input from:	Work Around/Non Value Added Step	Loss/Effect	Data To Gather	What is the analysis?	Who	Input Metric
		Are the inputs incomplete, late, wrong, missing?	How will it affect quality, time to market, cost effectiveness, capacity, or customer satisfaction? What will change if this problem was fixed?		What is the upstream step from which the input is provided?	What needs to be eliminated in future state?	What needs to be measured as a metric as baseline and ongoing to measure progress? What data do we have to measure the volume and overall effect of the problem today?	Source of data, unit of measure, stratification available (e.g. by industry), sampling approaches	Costs, quality, cycle time, customer dissatisfaction	Who would be engaged to gather the data	What data do we have to measure the volume and overall effect of the problem today? (input metric)
Concept	Inputs	Lack of insight to new technology trends.	Causes switch of technology later.	Medium	2.1 Process	Rework based on new technology.	Rework of technology. Contacting OM to get input.				
Concept	Indentify the required technologies.	Lack domain knowledge to meet requirements.	Proceed with what we know and then switch in later phase. This results in us driving to incorrect outputs of phase and if not caught later will drive rework in actual development.	Medium	Define high-level product concept.	Proceed with what we know.	% of projects with rework due to changes in technology decisions. % of hours in rework that are attributed to technology.	Product manager indicated they have examples of this.			
Plan	Outputs	Training/documentation plans not consistently completed. Tools for documentation not consistent across	Documentation may occur late in cycle or not at all.	High	Planning Process		% products produced without all levels of needed technical documentation/training collateral.				

Product Development Process

Conceptualize	Plan	Develop	Deploy

Conceptualize

- Evaluate performance of existing products/services against market opportunities
- Identify potential improvements to existing products and services
- Identify potential newproducts and services
  - Perform discovery research
  - Identify new technologies
  - Develop new technologies
  - Assess feasibility of integrating new leading technologies into product/service concepts
- Confirm alignment of product/service concepts with business strategy
  - Plan and develop cost and quality targets
  - Prioritize and select new product/service concepts
  - Specify development timing targets
  - Plan for product/service offering modifications

Plan

- Introduce newproducts/services
- Retire outdatedproducts/services
- Identify and refine performance indicators
- Assign resources to product/service project
- Prepare high-level business case and technical assessment

Develop

- Develop product/service design specifications
- Document design specifications
- Conduct mandatory and elective external reviews (legal, regulatory, standards, internal)
- Build prototypes
- Eliminate quality and reliability problems
- Conduct in-house product/service testing and evaluate feasibility
- Identify design/development performance indicators
- Collaborate design with suppliers and contract manufacturers
- Test market for new or revised products and services
- Prepare detailed market study
- Conduct customer tests and interviews
- Finalize product/service characteristics and business cases
- Finalize technical requirements
- Identify requirements for changes to manufacturing/delivery processes

Deploy

- Prepare for production
- Develop and test prototype production and/or service delivery process
- Design and obtain necessary materials and equipment
- Install and validate production process or methodology

(Continued)

123

What is the function you are reviewing?	What is the process you are reviewing?	Are the inputs incomplete, late, wrong, missing?	How will it affect Quality, Time to Market, Cost Effectiveness, Capacity, or Customer Satisfaction? What will change if this problem was fixed?	What is the extent of the impact?
Risk Area	Process	Issue	Risk or Impact	Impact Rating
Conceptualize	Inputs	Lack of insight into new technology trends	Causes switch of technology later	Medium
Conceptualize	Indentify the required technologies	Lack domain knowledge to meet requirements	Proceed with what we know and then switch in us driving to incorrect outputs of phase and if not caught later will drive rework in actual development.	Medium
Plan	Establish 3rd party agreements	SLA for support on software (SW) is not being done consistently. Calls come into Customer Service (CS) where the agreements do not cover needs for support.	Issue is we may not get support from customer or incur incremental costs	High
Plan & Develop	All	Multiple and non-integrated tools used within the process and different between each offer team.	The inefficiency in this process is everywhere and a major pain point!	Very High
Develop	Develop Product	Code reuse isn't happening and thus we are incurring extra development costs and slowing our time to market.	Slow time to market, process waste	High
Develop	Outputs	SW configuration process not consistently used and SW versions for financial SW are not aligned to unique SW PIDs.	Cannot support SW in field as there was no configuration management control from end-to-end. Handoffs from group to group result in modifications to software and without modification controls can ingest errors. Patch application may occur on an incorrect or non-certified version.certified version.	High
Deploy	Software (SW)Distribution	No standard process for SW archiving and distribution	Delays in revenue recognition due to not being able to download. Different processes to distribute SW.	Medium

Continued from Risks

What is the function you are reviewing?	What is the upstream step from which the input is provided	What is the upstream step from which the input is provided	What metric needs to be captured as a baseline as well as on an ongoing basis to measure progress? What data do we have to help us measure the volume and overall effect of the problem today?
Risk Area	Input from:	Work Around / Non Value Added Step	Loss/Effect Conceptualize
Conceptualize	2.1 Process	Rework based on new technology	Rework of technology
Plan		Secure agreement on development resources	% of escalations to CS where we cannot get support from third parties or where incremental costs are incurred. $ value of incremental cost incurred because SLA was not properly negotiated. % of times a non-standard agreement is used to negotiate SLAs.
Plan &Develop	Full process	Development cycle	% of lost productivity in engineering function. % of offers which cannot be supported because of having to go to different tools for information.
Develop	Development cycle	React to issues as they control	$ lost productivity when problems/patches have to be addressed. % of SW stacks that have been imaged in the field or managed in local databases and not available in SW configurationprocess. SW Build time improved by consolidating process/tools to a larger central server.
Deploy			% of SW that is remotely transmitted versus transmitted in a manual fashion.

(Continued)

125

What is the function you are reviewing?	Source of data, unit of measure, stratification available (e.g. by industry), sampling approaches	Costs, quality, cycle time, customer dissatisfaction.	Who would be engaged to gather the data?	What data do we have to measure the volume and overall effect of the problem today? (input metric)
Risk Area	Data To Gather	What is the analysis ?	Who	Input Metric
Conceptualize				
Conceptualize	Product Manager indicated they have examples of this.			
Plan	Customer Service team would be a source of input for part of this and Procurement for the rest of this.			
Plan & Develop	Source code control, resquests for service, documentation, etc. all in one system. May need to do some sampling.			
Develop				
Develop	Issues here is that we need to have a global data base of software configurations that exist by site so we can support it globally regardless of who modified the code last.	Point on this risk is that we need to standardize on a SW configuration process that supports the enterprise.		
Deploy				

Continued from Issues

Risks/Issues	Measure Type	Unit of Measurement	Related conditions to record	Sampling notes	Data Source	Data Request
SW updates/patches provided for non maintenance customers	Discreet	%, year, $	2007-2008, offer, application, region	Need to understand total number of patches loaded a year against HW maintenance contracts. Recommend samples over last 2 years	Customer Service (CS) system	In CS system extract fields for previous 2 yrs: •Date of service call •Reason code = "SW" or "SW Patch" •Warranty or Maintenance Customer = "no" •Any fields related to number of visits or time spent by tech.
Products released without technical documentation and training completed	Discreet	%, #	Offer, product, Software (SW), hardware (HW)	Customer Service (CS) may have tracked this issue.	Technical training system Technical documentation system	Products released system: Capture the following fields for previous 2 yrs: •Type of Product (product released ID #) •Release date •Tollgate approval fields (specifically any tech doc date/completion field). Technical documentation system: Parse into the previous file by product released ID # the following fields: •Date tech documentation created •individual that created documentation. Training system : Parse into data file by product released ID#: •Courses offered •Date of course, individuals who took course •Date the individual completed course.

spent all this time preparing so you can identify your root cause projects; make sure they are data driven.

And if you have an issue with someone who wants to jump the gun, just keep saying "Show me the data!" The Six Sigma methodology and tools are probably the best ones to use for any improvement project, but you may also find Lean and 5S valuable, especially for supply chain and manufacturing projects. Lean is an initiative to remove all waste from your manufacturing processes.[2] 5S is a Japanese concept of housekeeping, which, when applied to business, suggests that companies follow the five "S" steps: sort, straighten, shine, standardize, and sustain. Because you can learn about the Six Sigma process at any decent business improvement website, I've omitted it from this discussion.

We've made it through the first half of the BPI effort. The second half is standard project management and execution, which you should fold into your current CI program. Project charters are completed, projects are prioritized, and teams are formed to start working on the improvements. You may need to use a combination of tools to help solve the problems in your processes, like Lean, 5S, Theory of Constraints, and Six Sigma. If you don't have trained experts or certified Master Black Belts/Black Belts, then do yourself a favor and hire some, either through consulting firms or permanently. They are extremely valuable and helpful during this entire restructuring effort, which can be long and hard without the right resources.

It is important to monitor your financial savings/investments for each project and also have a summary for each category and Level 2 processes. These figures will feed into the overall restructuring effort financial savings template that the Steering Committee and CEO review weekly.

As your organization tweaks, reengineers, and/or automates processes, make sure that there are clear owners of the Level 3 subprocesses whose pay is tied to process performance. This is critical to long-term success. Metrics should be implemented for all

Level 3 subprocesses, and they should be monitored weekly. If there is an issue, metrics will capture it quickly so resolution can occur quickly as well.

BPI can seem intimidating and difficult on its own, but when paired with a restructuring effort, it can appear overwhelming. The easy steps in Exhibit 6.19 can help you tackle it without worry of missing something. And as your organizations change during the effort, through downsizing or product realignment, it is important to revisit your process maps and adjust them.

Continuing to put the customer first, consistently monitoring your metrics, and always looking for process improvement opportunities will keep you ahead of the game, providing a competitive and a cost advantage.

Business Process Outsourcing

The third workstream is Business Process Outsourcing BPO, which also works simultaneously with the BPI and OE workstream. The BPO team consists of a leader with very strong outsourcing or sourcing expertise, and subject matter experts from the functions or domains that have been highlighted in the original assessment discussed in Chapter 1. Like the BPI team, the BPO team is several layers down in the organization, usually layers 3 and 4, and consists of the people who own the activities being reviewed for potential outsourcing. The role of this team is to capture the information required to execute the activities in the workstream and to build the business case that will permit the leadership team to make the right decisions about outsourcing or keeping it in house.

Exhibit 6.19 shows the standard process steps used to secure an outsourcing vendor. As with Organizational Efficiency or Business Process Improvement, BPO is a practice and a discipline. Very few companies have the expertise in-house. This is a very specialized skill, and managing the process may require help from an external firm.

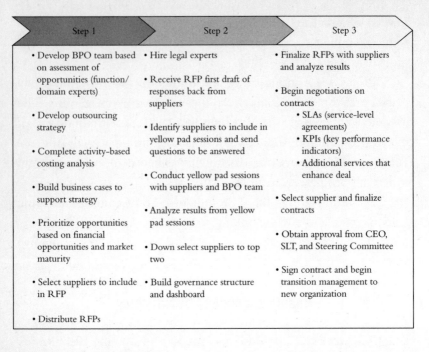

Exhibit 6.19 BPO Process

The first step for the BPO workstream is to review the original assessment and the output from the OE Business Core Competency Model with team members to identify the functions or domain areas where you can achieve financial benefits from outsourcing or offshoring. Typical functions that are mature in the market and frequently outsourced include:

- Finance and accounting
- Information technology
- Human resources
- Real estate
- Procurement

Additionally, you must review of the business strategy and current technology platforms in order to develop the outsourcing strategy, which will be the road map for how you will achieve the financial opportunities.

There are three inputs into the outsourcing strategy:

1. Results of a detailed activity-based costing survey for each process (Such a survey must be conducted using the team member and the process owners in the business.)
2. The BCCM output (specifically the activities that were plotted in the shared services category)
3. The standard and mature processes that generally are out-sourced in the market

These inputs are analyzed and a business case is built outlining the financial and operation benefits of outsourcing. This is the point when the company has to decide which activities you are going to go to market with in a request for proposal (RFP), and to which suppliers you will send the RFP.

The answer to "Who is the right supplier for my company to partner with?" depends on several variables. What you are trying to achieve with the outsourcing effort? If it is strictly cost, then you may decide to send the RFP to Tier 2 vendors. If you are looking for cost and an enterprise-wide process and technology platform, then you may decide Tier 1 players are the correct choice.

The answer to "How many suppliers should I send RFPs to?" again depends on the strategy you are executing, but no more than five or six.

The RFP process is long and involved. Trying to do it yourself will not reap the same results as using an external advisor. The advisor knows the market data and pricing and will be able to negotiate the best deal while ensuring you get key performance indicators that align to your strategy map and balanced scorecard. Additionally, the contracts are complex and can be hundreds of pages, so having a good external outsourcing law firm, working with your BPO advisor, representing you is critical.

Once you have sent the RFP, the next stage is the yellow pad sessions, where the suppliers come in and demonstrate their strength in the function or domain they are bidding on. This is where the BPO team and the leadership get to view the supplier's tools, processes, and management and the supplier gets to ask questions that will help it price the RFP.

Once these sessions are complete, the suppliers send back the RFP with their bid to the BPO Leader. At this point, it is critical to know the price of the most recent deal in the market. Negotiations occur for weeks and months until you select the top two suppliers and basically complete the RFP process.

The next step is to down select to two companies you want to enter contract negotiations with.

> **Quick Tip**
>
> ☞ Always have two companies you select so you have good negotiating power. Large outsourcers will try to convince you to do a sole source deal, which is only an advantage to them. Competitive bids will only occur if there are two or more suppliers making it to the final round of contract negotiations.

At this point hand things over to the lawyers. A company lawyer will not have the insight and expertise to do these negotiations alone, so hire a specialist firm. Ensuring you get the full benefit the supplier can offer is an added bonus that you get when you hire a law firm that has expertise in outsourcing.

If the supplier has continuous improvement in-house, ask for a productivity gain year over year on the processes. If it has consulting in-house, ask for help setting up the governance structure for the outsourcing contract. Knowing what to ask for and what you can partner with the supplier on in addition to the contract will build a better return on investment for you and lead to a more rewarding relationship.

The final step is the transition of the organization and processes over to the supplier. There will be an overlap period during which you will be conducting the processes and the supplier will, to make sure nothing falls between the cracks. At one point, you will cut over to the supplier completely, leaving a retained organization that will be working on only these activities the outsourcer did not take on. This is where OE is iterative, and conducts a mini-Work-Out to build the right structure to the support the new business model and retained organization model. It is very important that the project leader from OE, whom we discussed earlier, is managing the transition, including the business continuity risk, along with the Risk Management Leader from the PMO.

Because of the complexity and confusion most companies have regarding outsourcing, I asked a BPO expert Kaushik Bhaumik from Cognizant, one of the leading outsourcing firms in the world, to take you through the advantages of outsourcing and the trends in the market today.

Business Process Outsourcing as a Key Enabler for Restructuring

Kaushik Bhaumik, Ph.D.

Vice President and Global Practice Leader,
Business Process Outsourcing,
Cognizant Technology Solutions

Over the past decade, CEOs at companies large and small have taken a fundamental look at their business operations and asked themselves two key questions:

1. Which business processes is my company truly distinctive at and play a considerable role in value-add to my customers? (These are core processes.)
2. Which processes are important to my business, but my company is not necessarily better at executing those processes than anyone else? (These are noncore processes.)

These framing questions, often referred to as the core versus noncore debate, have been at the root of the tremendous growth of the role of business process outsourcing over the past several years. For this discussion, we limit our scope of BPO to non-manufacturing-related activities (industry-specific back-office work, finance/accounting, human resources administration, research/development, analytics-related activities, and transaction processing).

Through innovations in technology connectivity, process work flow automation, and the availability of highly skilled labor pools in lower-cost regions of the world (e.g., India, China, Latin America, Eastern Europe), the BPO industry has grown over 30 percent per year over the past five years to a $200 billion industry in 2007.[3] The bulk of these industry revenues are associated with same geography BPO (i.e., domestic outsourcing). However, the fastest-growing segment of outsourcing is associated with offshoring (moving processes to lower-cost regions).

Industries across the spectrum, from banking, healthcare, insurance, retail, to telecommunications, have utilized the services of BPO firms so that they can focus on their core value-add processes. Many have done so to facilitate major corporate restructuring and, in the process, have reaped compelling hard and soft benefits:

- Immediate cash flow improvement
- Greater business agility and flexibility
- Improved strategic positioning

In this section we walk through each of these areas and discuss the key issues and actions that CEOs need to consider, so that their restructuring programs can take full advantage of what BPO has to offer. We will illustrate these benefits with examples from our client work at Cognizant Technology Solutions, across a spectrum of industries, and highlight specific management challenges faced.

Immediate Cash Flow Improvement

Often with corporate restructuring, cash-flow improvement is at the top of the CEO's agenda, in order to pay down debt, fund restructuring activities, and generate employee incentives. One of the greatest benefits of the newest generation of BPO, based on labor arbitrage, is the immediacy of impact. In previous decades, where BPO was largely confined to movement of activities to providers within the same geography, most benefits were based on gaining access to the provider's scale and improved productivity. These scale and productivity benefits typically accrued over many years and made the case for BPO challenging for companies in more trying circumstances of a restructuring.

With labor arbitrage, it possible to see cost savings in the range of 30 to 60 percent off baseline costs within six months of the completion process transition from company in-house services to an outsourced provider. These costs savings are possible with direct cost line items (e.g., transaction processing, industry-specific back office work) and also SG&A cost line items (finance/accounting, human resources administration, analytical support). For the purposes of a restructuring, it is vital to go through a rigorous, but quick, process portfolio assessment for outsourcing. Here senior management intervention will be required, as it will be a natural tendency for in-house process owners and leaders to argue against outsourcing on the basis of critical knowledge retention, possible customer satisfaction degradation, or risks to the overall operations. Our experience suggests that more processes can be outsourced than not and that CEOs and operations leaders need to push on

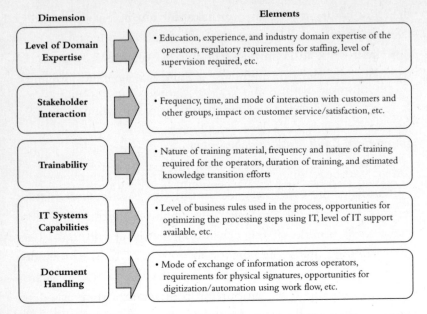

Exhibit 6.20 Key Dimensions to Assess Process Suitability for Outsourcing

the assumptions as to why certain processes need to be retained in-house. In Exhibit 6.20, we lay out a set of dimensions we have found helpful in clarifying for clients those processes that can be outsourced. The higher an individual process rates along each of these dimensions, the better suited it is for outsourcing.

Quickly capturing the savings associated with outsourcing will require some sensitive actions around reductions in force and staff redeployment. Simply speaking, without these actions, the immediate impact of the BPO business case evaporates. Therefore, it is important to have in place a change management program that carefully oversees the people and transition elements of an outsourcing program. The key elements of a BPO change management program are:

- **Transition plan.** Documents the approach toward transitioning process knowledge, customer needs, requirements and work

136

flow within the client organization from its current in-house configuration to a outsource partner.

- **Communication program.** A common set of messages for the outsourcing program that are delivered through executive workshops, memos, and Web to reinforce the business rationale for outsourcing and the steps your organization is taking to mediate impact to affected employees.
- **Organization structure redesign.** Reorganize the internal workforce to change focus from internal delivery management to outsource partner management, key customer interactions, and service-level management.

The up-front knowledge transition associated with BPO typically has both internal as well as outsource partner execution costs. With larger BPO programs, it is often possible to amortize these costs over the life of an outsourcing contract, providing more cash flexibility to the restructuring organization. Furthermore, the outsourcing partners sometimes are willing to recoup their transition costs by bundling them into the price of services rendered (which are often hourly resource based or transaction based). Transaction-based pricing is recommended after 6 to 12 months of outsourcing, to create a more flexible operating structure that can be modulated with swings in your end customer demand (see the next section).

As an example of the key elements of a successful outsourcing program focused on cash flow improvement, we discuss Cognizant's work with a leading video and gaming rental organization that is going through a significant corporate restructuring to respond to fundamental changes in its business (e.g., rise of on-demand video for personal computers and cable TV). These changes were resulting in a significant fall-off in consumer traffic to the retail outlets, so much so that the company needed to reduce operating costs very quickly (within six months). One cost area of focus was retail outlet support. This company has several hundred retail outlets, each requiring live, 24×7 store support to respond to staff issues and queries associated with the merchandising and point-of-sale systems. The company worked with Cognizant to outsource the support handling of these systems and, in doing so, was able to realize over 40 percent savings on those costs just through the immediate outsourcing. In addition, Cognizant has been able to introduce productivity gains, through centralization, better work flow and call queuing, that has provided another 10 percent savings. The company has redirected some of these savings to fund its own direct-to-consumer video and game initiatives, to better position itself in the rapidly changing consumer entertainment space.

Greater Business Agility and Flexibility

Beyond financial performance improvement, BPO is utilized to provide greater operational agility and flexibility to organizations. BPO makes it possible to tap into operations capabilities on an as-needed basis, without incurring start-up, fixed costs, and management hassles, through these levers:

- **Transaction-based pricing.** Getting charged on a unit of work (e.g., invoice processed, call handled, etc) allows companies to variablize previously fixed costs.
- **Volume-based arrangements.** Because the BPO provider has vastly more scale, it is possible to create an operations cost structure that gains from economies of scale, with pricing that declines with greater volumes.
- **Technology-enabled BPO (i.e., platform BPO).** Some more standardized business processes (e.g., expense reporting) lend themselves to a common technology platform that the BPO partner can provide to its clients, along with the services associated with that process.
- **Geographically distributed contingency workforces.** If your company goes through seasonal spikes or ebbs of work, BPO partners can provide temporary workforces to address those spikes on an as-needed basis

In the 2008–2009 economic climate of high demand uncertainty, such a set of arrangements can be invaluable to a company working its way through restructuring.

Our work with a leading global financial asset manager illustrates the use of some of these levers for improved business agility. This organization had challenges recruiting and maintaining an experienced workforce to handle the accounting and management of its $1.3 trillion worth of alternative investments (e.g., hedge funds). Furthermore, business complexities necessitated that the accounting occur on a near-real-time basis, such that investment positions would be updated and monitored 24×5. Cognizant established a center of over 200 accountants highly experienced in complex financial instruments and introduced technology and work flow to effectively pass the book of investments across the client's center in New York, Europe, and India, such that the objectives of 24×5 continuous investment management were met. Doing so, the client effectively globalized its workforce, without going through the challenges of setting up its own captive center in India.

Another example for BPO for flexibility is our service to a leading healthcare payor organization. Managing and paying claims is one of the most cost- and time-consuming activities for healthcare insurance companies. Often a fair amount of fraud occurs, as end patients and sometime providers (e.g., physicians) submit false or fraudulent claims, which end up driving up healthcare insurance premiums for all members. Cognizant worked with a payor to identify new aberrant billing patterns (ABPs) submitted by providers in their bills. It was discovered that a number of ABPs occurred in claims valued under $500, a segment that the payor had previously ignored and just paid out, as the costs of reviewing such low-value claims exceeded the claim payout. Through cost-effective outsourcing, Cognizant identified over 25 new fraud patterns that have saved the payor over $20 million annually in fraudulent claims payouts. This added flexibility of addressing previously ignored work or customer segments is a highly valued element of outsourcing.

Improved Strategic Positioning

Finally, BPO can be a valuable lever for fundamentally improving a restructured organization's strategic positioning for the longer term. Any CEO involved in a corporate restructuring knows that a strategic repositioning (in terms of markets/segments served, services/products developed and sold, geographies) is often a parallel set of activities to tactical financial or operational reengineering. Utilizing BPO along this vein requires viewing an outsourcing partner as an extension of your own organization, but with greater scale, capabilities, and reach than you may be able to build on your own. We have seen instances where an outsourcing partner provides avenues for geographic expansion, to carry out more core business processes (e.g., research and development [R&D]) and new product/service joint ventures, to reduce the risk on a restructured firm.

As an example of BPO for improved strategic positioning, Cognizant has been working with one of the world's leading pharmaceutical organizations to dramatically improve its product time to market and pipeline. One of the major strategic challenges facing all pharmaceutical organizations is the cost and time associated with bringing a new drug to market, which averages nearly $900 million and 10 years of research and development. One of the key activities within the clinical research value chain is known as clinical data management (CDM), a very intense, complex, and laborious task of managing all data that comes out of drug clinical trials, statistically analyzing the data for relevant efficacy trends, and submitting the information to regulatory authorities (e.g., U.S. Food and Drug Administration). This particular CDM engagement began in 2007 and has fundamentally transformed the client's clinical operations by centralizing and streamlining its clinical data management operations, improved process standardization, consistency of delivery, and economies of scale. The client has reinvested the savings associated with this more efficient CDM organization to support accelerated development of its R&D programs. Some of the key measures of improvement include:

- Delivered approximately 50 percent reduction in operating costs and improved R&D cycle times by over 20 percent.
- Study setup time cut by over 50 hours per study.
- Twenty percent reduction in quality control time for submitted data sets.

For an industry where new product research and development is its lifeblood, this kind of strategic relationship and results are an example that outsourcing can be significantly much more than cost savings.

Summary

BPO offers a variety of tools and levers to assist any organization through a restructuring. More and more organizations have found that BPO can catalyze their restructuring timelines and prospects through a more competitive cost structure, flexible operations, and by enabling key strategic growth initiatives.

Notes

1. Jack Welch and Robert Slater, *The G.E. Way: Management Insights and Leadership Secrets of the Legendary CEO* (New York: McGraw-Hill, 1998).

2. www.isixsigma.com/dictionary/glossary.asp.

3. "Capturing Opportunities in the Evolving Business Process Offshoring Marketplace," NASSCOM-Everest India BPO Study (March 2008).

Chapter 7

Leadership Essentials for Success

Do You Have What It Takes?

So far, we have talked about how to set up, organize, and execute a restructuring effort using a framework methodology, processes, and tools that have been proven in the market. We have demonstrated the importance of change management and communications as a vehicle to enable the changes that will occur and build an organization that understands the criticality of what the restructuring project will deliver. We discussed briefly in Chapter 3 the necessity of having a leadership team that will be supporters of the effort and act as change advocates to ensure that employees see the commitment from the top. But what we have not addressed yet are the team dynamics of the project team and the leadership team, and how this can significantly affect the results of the project. You can appoint the smartest, most competent people from your company on the team, but if the team dynamics are not effective, then you will have a more difficult time reaching your restructuring objectives, or any objectives for that matter.

In this chapter, we explore the value of building a team that combines the natural skills to deliver on a project like the one you are implementing. First, we look at the Keirsey® Temperament Sorter® (KTS®-II), an assessment that we utilize to better understand people's innate skills and how to use them for maximum advantage. To do so, I have asked Edward Kim to define and describe the approach, results, and insights the Keirsey methodology and tools convey. I find the methodology absolutely fascinating, so much so, that I and several members of my team became certified in Keirsey. One of my consultants put it wisely: Keirsey is to people the way physics is to the outside environment. As you can describe gravity, you can describe why someone is better at performing a task than someone else. There is a natural order. Now it is time to understand the natural order of people's abilities, and how they work together well . . . or not.

Plans versus People

Edward Kim

Managing Director,
Synergy Leaders, LLC

If you have thoroughly studied the first six chapters of this book, I believe that you just might have a chance at creating a near-perfect playbook for restructuring (or at least a playbook that has a much better chance of working than if you had not read this book)—thanks to Carla and her team at NexGen. It is often after reading books like this one, which outline steps to creating a more efficient strategic process or system, that we forge onward feeling inspired and intelligent enough to create/re-create our ideal organization. And if having that perfect playbook was all that is required, then this chapter would not be necessary.

This chapter focuses on the people side of your restructuring efforts. We at Synergy Leaders believe that in every restructuring effort, there is something we like to call "the People Factor." In our research, we have discovered the truth that organizational effectiveness disseminates not from having the *best strategies* but from having the *best people*; it is about having effective leaders, and teams with the right talents, lined up with strategic priorities, each playing roles that align their unique personalities to the task at hand. Brilliant *plans* do not lead to success; *people* who execute brilliant plans led an organization toward success. And conversely, when plans fail, it is because somewhere behind the plan were people who led an organization toward its demise. (Either because *people* poorly executed or *people* poorly planned.) At the end of the day, it all boils down to the people you have or do not have on your team. The multimillion-dollar strategic plan fails because you do not have the right people to pull it off. Because most organizations do not spend enough time assessing their talent mix, they often need to go outside the organization to pay for strategic plans. The truth is, if the organization had invested in assessing the talent mix of their people, it probably would have made sure that the team already had people with strategic planning capabilities in the first place, which could have saved millions of dollars on plans.

The saying that "people are an organization's greatest asset" has become a cliché, yet if you ask most organizational leaders whether they believe this statement, most would profess that they do so wholeheartedly. In practice, however, we find that very few leaders actually understand how to align the people within their organization for success. What often happens is that leaders spend exorbitant amounts of money and time coming up with the perfect plan.

Because of this, it seems that some leaders would rather keep the expensive plan in its flawless, untouched, sacred state rather than see it fail because of the people who get involved and mess it up. After paying the strategy consultants for the master plan, admiration for the plan sets in, but secretly those who have been around the block enough times will think to themselves, "Wow, this is such a brilliant plan! If only the plan didn't have to involve our people!"

So what comes first? The chicken or the egg? Do you start with *the plan* or *the people*? This is a tough question to answer. You will find experts on both sides of the fence putting forth their arguments. So rather than try to settle this issue here in this chapter, what we would like to put forth is that when considering your restructuring efforts, at some point (whether it is first or second), it is absolutely imperative that you do an assessment of your people's natural talents and an assessment of the configuration of your team dynamics. It is the only way to assess whether you will be able to pull off the restructur*ing*, and it is the only way to assess whether you have the right leaders to lead the restructur*ed* organization.

Keirsey Temperament Sorter

How do you assess the natural talents of your organization? And also, how do you assess the interaction dynamics of teams within your organization? In order to answer this question, we want to shift gears to try to understand people in a way similar to how we have been studying an organization. That is, through a framework methodology or a systems lens. All organizations are complex systems. Likewise, people are complex systems. And teams are complex systems. If we take a look at people and the structuring of teams through a similar perspective as we have been doing with organizational restructuring, we will begin to see that there are ways to systematically understand the configurations of individual talent and team dynamics.

146

Just as there are both use*ful* and use*less* models that exist for understanding organizational systems, there are many models for understanding human behavior that are both use*ful* and use*less*. Some models are highly theoretical and complicated, while there are some that are practical, applicable, and have stood the test of time.

The model we will introduce herein is one designed by renowned psychologist and best-selling author Dr. David Keirsey. Since its introduction, in his book *Please Understand Me*[1] (4 million sold), the Keirsey Temperament Sorter (KTS-II) has been taken by more than 40 million people in more than 170 different countries. Individuals and teams from more than two-thirds of the Fortune 500 companies have utilized the KTS-II for leadership development, team building, and organizational strategy.

First, let me provide you with the framework for Dr. Keirsey's model. Understanding this framework will have profound implications on how you would structure a team to lead your restruc*turing* efforts and how you would structure a team to lead the restructur*ed* organization. Keirsey's "Four Temperaments" are referred to as *Artisans*®, *Guardians*®, *Idealists*®, and *Rationals*®. These four temperaments can be further subdivided into what often are referred to as "Character Types." What this means is that there are 4 types of Artisans, 4 types of Guardians, 4 types of Idealists, and 4 types of Rationals, making up a total of 16 character types.[2] (See Exhibit 7.1.)

To find out the talent mix on your team, the first step is to figure out which types of people are on your team. By using the KTS-II personality instrument, individuals and teams can work this out. The KTS-II is a powerful 70-question assessment that helps individuals discover their personality type (i.e., Rational-Fieldmarshal-ENTJ, or Guardian-Protector-ISFJ).

The questions in the KTS-II are designed to sort between four dichotomous pairs of preferences, leading to results that reveal a person's temperament and character type. Exhibit 7.2 outlines the four preference scales which a respondent would choose between.

ARTISAN	GUARDIAN	IDEALIST	RATIONAL
Promoter (ESTP)	Supervisor (ESTJ)	Teacher (ENFJ)	Fieldmarshal (ENTJ)
Crafter (ISTP)	Inspector (ISTJ)	Counselor (INFJ)	Mastermind (INTJ)
Performer (ESFP)	Provider (ESFJ)	Champion (ENFP)	Inventor (ENTP)
Composer (ISFP)	Protector (ISFJ)	Healer (INFP)	Architect (INTP)

Exhibit 7.1   4 Temperaments and 16 Character Types

HISTORICAL TERMS	MEANING		HISTORICAL TERMS	MEANING
Extroversion (E)	Expressive	vs.	Introversion (I)	Attentive
Sensing (S)	Observant	vs.	Intuiting (N)	Introspective
Thinking (T)	Tough-minded	vs.	Feeling (F)	Friendly
Judging (J)	Scheduled	vs.	Perceiving (P)	Probing

Exhibit 7.2   4 Preference Scales

Once individuals figure out their temperament/character type, we have the relevant data to move forward in structuring the team in such a way that communication can be optimized, natural talent can be leveraged, and effective leadership can take place, whether it is for restructur*ing* or for leading a restructur*ed* organization. A team comprised of mostly Guardians, for example, will behave differently from a team comprised of mostly Rationals. Whether a team is heavily comprised of one type over another or a team is comprised of a wide mixture of different types, each team's configuration has certain dynamics that are present. And based on the configuration of the team, there are certain opportunities that a team may be better leveraged for and certain challenges that a team will inevitably encounter because of the team makeup. When it comes to people's values, inclinations, communication, action, and talents, six decades of our research indicates that there are hard-wired patterns for these various dimensions.

It is important to note that finding each person's unique type is not the end goal. It is simply a means to an end. In other words, you find out the natural wiring patterns of team members *so that* you can figure out what roles each person can effectively play. Most teams/organizations have utilized personality assessments before, but not in the ways that we are suggesting. For the most part, these types of assessments are utilized as a fun exercise to get to know each other. We suggest that this is literally only the tip of the iceberg. It should not just end with self/mutual understanding. The understanding gained ought to be utilized for action, to effect strategic outcomes.

As we proceed, there are some fundamental assumptions we are making about people (which you may or may not agree with). For argument's sake, if you would at least consider these assumptions for a moment as truth, we feel that it will lead to a place where you will be positioned to see the massive iceberg beneath the water's surface. Keirsey doctrine in its purest form can be summarized in three doctrines:

1. People are different from each other. (We differ from each other in fundamental ways).
2. No amount of getting after someone is going to change him or her. Nor is there any reason to change the person because the differences are probably good.
3. Differences are all around us and are not difficult to see, if we look.

The implications for restructuring and organizational leadership follow accordingly. The implication of the first doctrine is that (1) *certain leaders will have certain talents that are either a fit or not a fit to lead a restructuring effort or a restructured organization.* The implication of the second doctrine is that (2) *changing a leader to fit into a role he or she is not naturally wired for is a waste of time and energy.* And finally, the implication of the third doctrine is that (3) *if we take the time to assess the natural wiring pattern of those on our teams, the more informed we will be to align the right people for the right roles—leading to maximum results.*

Implication 1: Certain Leaders Have Certain Talents

Looking at Exhibit 7.3, we should note that each of the four temperaments have different natural talents. Artisans have *Tactical* intelligence; Guardians have *Logistical* intelligence; Idealists have *Diplomatic* intelligence; and Rationals have *Strategic* intelligence. And each of the 16 character types has a specific talent that can be viewed as a subset of the main type of intelligence.

So, for example, we would say that all Rationals have Strategic intelligence, and depending on which type of Rational you are, you would use that Strategic intelligence in different ways. The Fieldmarshal (one of the four Rationals), for example, uses strategic intelligence for *mobilizing* followers, while the Mastermind (another of the four Rationals), for example, uses strategic intelligence for *entailing* intricate contingency plans and complex systems.

ARTISAN *Tactical*	GUARDIAN *Logistical*	IDEALIST *Diplomatic*	RATIONAL *Strategic*
Promoter *persuading*	Supervisor *enforcing*	Teacher *educating*	Fieldmarshal *mobilizing*
Crafter *instrumenting*	Inspector *certifying*	Counselor *guiding*	Mastermind *entailing*
Performer *demonstrating*	Provider *supplying*	Champion *motivating*	Inventor *devising*
Composer *synthesizing*	Protector *securing*	Healer *conciliating*	Architect *designing*

Exhibit 7.3   Talents of the 4 Temperaments and 16 Character Types

What we are not saying is that each person is limited to only that area, but that in observing tens of thousands of individuals over the past six decades, we have seen that individuals who are a certain character type consistently displays talent in these specific areas in ways that are clearly head and shoulders above others who are not that particular type. Consider these four famous leaders: Donald Trump (Artisan-Promoter), Warren Buffett (Guardian-Inspector), Oprah Winfrey (Teacher-Idealist), and Steve Jobs (Rational-Inventor).

Donald Trump, as an Artisan-Promoter, is perhaps one of the most self-promotional leaders we have seen, able to convince anyone to get on board with his enterprise. He has a natural talent of *tactically persuading* his way through any negotiation. Warren Buffett as a Guardian-Inspector has a simple and straightforward approach to investing that has made him billions. He has a highly disciplined *logistical* approach, which provides him the ability to carefully inspect and accurately assess the value of an enterprise, *certifying* its worthiness for investment. Oprah Winfrey, as a Teacher-Idealist, has created a platform through which she teaches more people about more subjects than any other human being alive. She is a master of *diplomacy* whenever she conducts an interview. Through her natural talent, she ends up *educating* millions of people worldwide, by hosting a show where she addresses a wide range of topics, by reporting on leading-edge issues, or by inviting world-class experts to educate viewers on a daily basis. Steve Jobs, as a Rational-Inventor, uses his creative abilities to think outside the box. As a result of his *strategic devising* capabilities, he has introduced such inventions as the Mac, the iPod, and the iPhone.[3]

Implication 2: Changing a Leader to Fit

Could Warren Buffett do what Steve Jobs does (does Buffett even know how to use an iPod)? Or could Donald Trump be as successful as Oprah Winfrey as a talk-show host (would he even care to be)? The point is that there are areas where people have natural inclinations to be *brilliant, expert, great, good, average, below average*, and *incompetent*. Warren Buffett may be *incompetent* in *devising* innovative inventions, but that is okay, because he has other talents. And he has invested his efforts to be *brilliant* in his talent area. If you are *brilliant* in a certain area, you can put minimal effort into the utilization/development of that talent and get a huge return. If you are *incompetent* in a certain area, you would have to expend exorbitant amounts of energy to even get a small return.

When it comes to the idea of utilizing/developing one's talents, we have a principle we adhere to that we like to call the $1\times = 10\times/10\times = 1\times$ Principle. This principle basically states that if you invest *1 amount* of energy into developing and utilizing your most *natural talents*, you will get a *$10\times$ return* on that *small investment*. The converse is also true. You can spend *$10\times$ amount* of energy into utilizing/developing your most *unnatural talents*, and you will get a *$1\times$ return* on that *large investment*.

Donald Trump does not need to expend that much energy in utilizing/developing his tactical persuading skills to produce significant outcomes. In Trump's case (as an Artisan-Promoter) by personality type, his most opposite would be the Idealist-Healer. Someone like Albert Schweitzer or Princess Diana would be an Idealist-Healer. If Trump were to make attempts to utilize/develop diplomatic skills in "conciliating" others, could he do this? Perhaps he could, but could he be great, expert, or brilliant at it? We would argue that, first of all, he most likely would not even be interested in such activities, but if he were, and if he made substantial efforts to develop in this area, he would need to spend vast amounts of energy to make even a fraction of progress (compared to someone who already has natural talent) in this area. He could spend a great deal of energy in this arena and perhaps move from below average to becoming average or possibly good in this area, but never great, expert, or brilliant.

The great travesty of all this, however, would be that this type of investment presents a monumental "opportunity cost" for Trump. All of that time and energy spent in trying to be an Idealist-Healer is at the opportunity cost of time and energy he could otherwise be spending in areas in which he is predisposed to be brilliant, expert, or great. Aligning leaders who naturally fit well for certain outcomes is far easier than trying to change a leader to fit certain ends.

Implication 3: Assessing and Aligning for the Right Roles

Thus far, we have introduced you to the idea that different temperaments/character types have different talents. Unfortunately, talent is not the only factor we need to consider in the structuring of a team. In other words, you can make attempts to group a bunch of superstars together, each with brilliance in their respective talents, but would this ensure success? Would they know how to work together as a team? Say we were to put Donald Trump (Artisan), Mother Teresa (Guardian), Albert Einstein (Rational), Jack Welch (Rational), Oprah Winfrey (Idealist), Albert Schweitzer (Idealist), Elvis Presley (Artisan), and Warren Buffett (Guardian) all on the same team. No one could argue against the fact that we have an enormous amount of talent in this group. If we look closely, we would note that there is an equal representation of all four temperaments on this team (two Artisans, two Guardians, two Idealists, and two Rationals).

Many people may look at this team, and say, "Wow! What a team! This is ideal. We have all four talents covered. This team has tactical, logistical, diplomatic, and strategic brilliance!" If you were to reach this conclusion, you would be making a gross mistake. In assembling a team, whether it is for leading a restructuring effort or for leading the restructured organization, it is imperative to understand what the mission or end the team is trying to achieve. Assembling a team with the right talent mix for the mission is absolutely critical.[4]

If, for example, your enterprise is a strategy consulting firm, you will want to have a disproportionately high percentage of Rationals (whose strongest natural talent is strategic capabilities). It is not that the other temperaments and talents are not required. In fact, in any enterprise, you may have certain niche roles that require the natural talents of other temperaments. For example, in the case of the strategy consulting firm, you may have some Idealists present who excel at client relations (with their diplomatic talents), or Artisans who are great negotiators and sales executives (with their tactical talents). However, these are minor roles within this enterprise, as you can see in Exhibit 7.4.

If you are running a global retail operation and need to establish logistical procedures, processes, and rules, and you need people to follow protocol, you will want to have a disproportionately high percentage of Guardians (whose strongest natural talent is logistical capabilities), as in Exhibit 7.5.

Other enterprises, such as nonprofit humanitarian aid organizations, may have a disproportionately high percentage of Idealists, who have an innate desire to save the world, as seen in Exhibit 7.6.

A start-up enterprise like the one in Exhibit 7.7 may be filled with a disproportionately high percentage of Artisans who

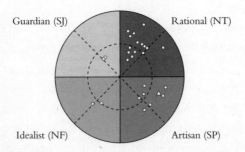

Exhibit 7.4 Sample Temperament Map 1: Strategy Consulting Firm
SOURCE: The Temperament Maps have been provided courtesy of Keirsey.com, and the cases herein are samples from Keirsey.com's consulting services division, Synergy Leaders, LLC.

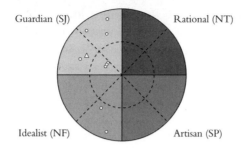

Guardian (SJ)　　　　　　　Rational (NT)

Idealist (NF)　　　　　　　Artisan (SP)

Exhibit 7.5　Sample Temperament Map 2: Retail Operations Team

SOURCE: The Temperament Maps have been provided courtesy of Keirsey.com, and the cases herein are samples from Keirsey.com's consulting services division, Synergy Leaders, LLC.

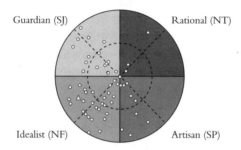

Guardian (SJ)　　　　　　　Rational (NT)

Idealist (NF)　　　　　　　Artisan (SP)

Exhibit 7.6　Sample Temperament Map 3: Humanitarian Aid Organization

SOURCE: The Temperament Maps have been provided courtesy of Keirsey.com, and the cases herein are samples from Keirsey.com's consulting services division, Synergy Leaders, LLC.

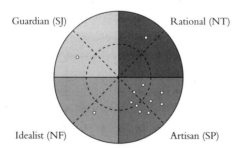

Guardian (SJ)　　　　　　　Rational (NT)

Idealist (NF)　　　　　　　Artisan (SP)

Exhibit 7.7　Sample Temperament Map 4: Entrepreneurial Start-up

SOURCE: The Temperament Maps have been provided courtesy of Keirsey.com, and the cases herein are samples from Keirsey.com's consulting services division, Synergy Leaders, LLC.

are great at tactical maneuvering and making things up as they go. The point is that you will want to consider what the mission at hand is and have the right people on board to achieve those objectives.

As you can see, different teams are configured differently, and certain configurations are perhaps better suited for certain objectives and/or industries. As the final consideration of this chapter, we turn to a brief case study, which has specific ramifications for how the People Factor in an organization matters.

Case Study: Can We Compete in This Arena?

The Client[5] Synergy Leaders had the opportunity to serve the organizational change management (OCM) practice within a large global consulting firm.

The Context The firm's OCM practice was at a pivotal moment. New leadership had been installed, and new considerations for the direction of the OCM practice were being discussed. The OCM practice had been effectively doing organizational change management for many years and had earned the reputation within the industry as being among the best at what they do. Under new leadership, considerations were being made to move into the strategy consulting arena with this group.

The Problem From our perspective, the key question was whether the practice was comprised of the right mix of people, with the right set of capabilities, to compete with some of the top strategy consulting firms in the world. Before investing millions of dollars into training, recruiting, and developing this new business, Keirsey. com provided an analysis for this practice, to find out whether the people were ready for this shift.

The Discovery Fifty-three consultants took the KTS-II, and these were the results:

34 consultants turned out to be Guardians (64.1 percent)
11 consultants turned out to be Idealists (20.8 percent)
5 consultants turned out to be Artisans (9.4 percent)
3 consultants turned out to be Rationals (5.7 percent)

Refer to Exhibit 7.8 to view the distribution.

The reason for the practice's superiority in its type of consulting was because it had the right people on board. The type of work that OCM consultants do requires a tremendous amount of logistical coordination, something that comes most naturally to Guardians. When we compared the talent makeup of this group against top strategy consulting firms, what we found was very eye opening. The top strategy consulting firms are comprised mostly of Rationals (who are most gifted in strategy and weakest in logistics). Strategy firms have the fewest number of Guardians, the temperament type that the OCM practice had in abundance. If we compare the temperament map of this firm's OCM consultants to the temperament map of consultants from a top strategy consulting firm, the picture is quite clear. Do a quick comparison between Exhibits 7.4 and 7.8 so that you can see for yourself.

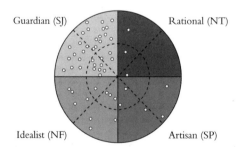

Guardian (SJ)   Rational (NT)

Idealist (NF)   Artisan (SP)

Exhibit 7.8 Case Study Temperament Map: OCM Consultants
SOURCE: The Temperament Maps have been provided courtesy of Keirsey.com, and the cases herein are samples from Keirsey.com's consulting services division, Synergy Leaders, LLC.

As you will note, the comparison shows how different this OCM consulting practice is compared to consultants from a top global strategy consulting firm. In working with Strategy Consulting firms throughout the world, we have found that in most cases, their temperament configuration consistently has an overwhelmingly high percentage of Rationals and very few Guardians.[6]

For the purposes of this chapter, we will end the case study here, but I think you understand what is quite obvious. In light of concepts we introduced throughout this chapter, you would not have to be a rocket scientist to know what we advised. If I were to ask you to bet large sums of money on the chances of the OCM practice restructur*ing* successfully into a restructur*ed* strategy consulting practice, how would you bet? It may seem silly to ask about how you would bet, but this is exactly what businesses are doing when they are considering restructuring their organizations. They are deciding how much to "invest" (bet) on the initiative. And in many cases, the People Factor is given very little consideration. From our research, we would strongly suggest that in any restructuring effort, before you decide to bet millions of dollars on a new strategic initiative, you do the work of assessing whether you have the right people to pull off the change and the right people to lead the newly created organization.

Notes

1. David Keirsey, *Please Understand Me II: Temperament, Character, Intelligence* (Del Mar, CA: Prometheus Nemesis Book Co., 1998).

2. If you are familiar with the Myers-Briggs letter combinations, you will notice in Exhibit 7.1 that the Myers-Briggs types coincide with Keirsey's model. There are some similarities as well as key differences (which we will not get into in this chapter). There is no affiliation between Keirsey and Myers-Briggs. (They are about as affiliated as Coke and Pepsi, or Mac and PC.)

3. A full treatment of how "different leaders lead differently" is addressed in the book by Edward J. Kim and David M. Keirsey, *Different Kinds of Leaders*. (from the Please Understand Me® series books).

4. For the purposes of this chapter, we will limit our discussion to the subject of aligning talent to mission. But there are other critical factors for assembling an effective team that need careful consideration. Other critical factors to understand are the *values, inclinations, communication* style, and *action* styles of the team members.

   Artisans value *stimulation/impact*, Guardians value *security/authority*, Idealists value *identity/intuition*, and Rationals value *knowledge/reason*. Artisans are inclined to live in *action* land, Guardians in *check-list* land, Idealists in *potential* land, and Rationals in *complexity* land.

   When it comes to Artisans and Guardians, both temperaments are *Concrete* in their *communication* (*Talk about Reality*), while Idealists and Rationals are *Abstract* in their *communication* (*Talk about Ideas*).

   When it comes to the *action* style of the four temperaments, Guardians and Idealists are *Cooperative* in their action (*Do What's Right*), while Artisans and Rationals are *Utilitarian* in their action (*Do What Works*).

5. The client shall remain anonymous, and minor details have been modified to ensure protection of the firm's identity. The principles and implications that can be learned from this case are identical had the case study been presented without any modifications.

6. The U.S. Population is comprised of approximately 30 percent Artisans, 45 percent Guardians, 15 percent Idealists, and 10 percent Rationals.

   Keirsey, Temperament Sorter, KTS, Please Understand Me, Guardian, Idaelist, Rational are registered trademarks and trademarks of Dr. David Keirsey. For more information on the use of these trademarks, please visit www.keirsey.com.

Chapter 8

Continuous Improvement

Moving from Conscious Competence to Unconscious Competence

You have finally reached the end of your restructuring project plan . . . but is it really the end? Heck, NO! Now comes the hard part of keeping the rhythm of continuous improvement going for long-term impact to your company. It is not really a program, because it never goes away, but it is not about fighting fires either! It is a way of operating your business that embeds quality into everything your employees do, from taking an order to making a product or providing a service to your customers.

One of the biggest mistakes we see companies make is to put time, energy, and resources into an initiative, only to have the benefits suboptimized because they lack the discipline to maintain the pace they exhibited during the project. In order for you to move

161

from "Conscious Competence"—meaning you know what needs to be done and how to do it—to "Unconscious Competence"—meaning you make improvements as a normal part of operating your business—you must implement Continuous Improvement (CI). The restructuring organization transitions to a continuous improvement organization, as in Exhibit 8.1.

As discussed in Chapter 1, restructuring is a practice you should perform every year to keep your competitive advantage. But in the meantime, you need to preserve and, it is hoped, improve the changes you implemented during the project in order to reap the financial and operational benefits you identified during the assessment phase.

How do you sustain and continuously improve your business? Several actions must be executed to safeguard your company from reverting back to the way it used to do things. Here is a list of the actions you will need to take in order to ensure you are able to sustain and continuously improve your business.

- **Commitment.** A commitment to improve your business will be required, but that starts at the top and is a given. However, making it clear by adding "Continuous Improvement mind-set" into your values, compensation, and performance ratings will go a long way to embed the methodology into your culture.
- **CI organization structure.** Identify a strong leader who will provide visibility to the CEO about how the business is operating. This structure builds an organization that will support the business and provide cost reduction and revenue/margin opportunities by using various quality methodologies.
- **CI dashboard.** As discussed in Chapter 4, a balanced scorecard is imperative to understand how the business is functioning. The CI dashboard is the means to measure business processes, including those managed by outside vendors.
- **Training: Six Sigma/Lean training for CEO, Senior Leadership Team (SLT), CI organization, and process owners.** The training will be different for each group but will

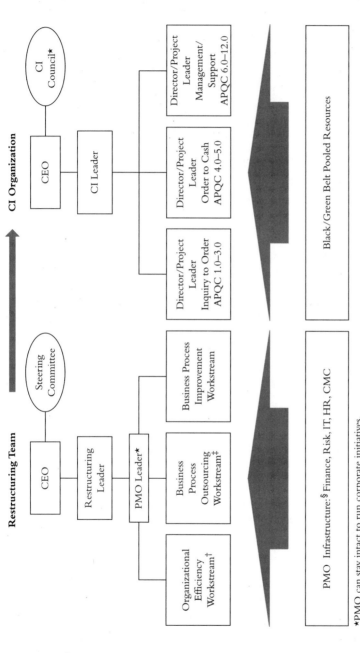

Restructuring Team

CEO — Restructuring Leader — PMO Leader★

Steering Committee

- Organizational Efficiency Workstream[†]
- Business Process Outsourcing Workstream[‡]
- Business Process Improvement Workstream

CI Organization

CEO — CI Leader

CI Council★

- Director/Project Leader Inquiry to Order APQC 1.0–3.0
- Director/Project Leader Order to Cash APQC 4.0–5.0
- Director/Project Leader Management/ Support APQC 6.0–12.0

PMO Infrastructure:[§] Finance, Risk, IT, HR, CMC

Black/Green Belt Pooled Resources

★PMO can stay intact to run corporate initiatives.
[§]PMO Infrastructure goes back to core function, but supports the CI organization.
[†]OE Workstream moves to organizational development group in HR.
[‡]BPO moves into governance structure with procurement.

Exhibit 8.1 Restructuring Team Transitions to Continuous Improvement Organization

be necessary in order for everyone to understand what, why, and how improvements will be made.

- **Knowledge management.** Use a knowledge management database to house processes, documents, tools, and best practices to be shared with the organization. Also use a knowledge transfer document and tool kit to capture knowledge from external experts to leadership and process owners on how to execute future changes in their area of expertise.

Continuous Improvement is a management process that focuses on processes the customer sees as value added. Processes are assessed continually and then changed or improved to make them the most efficient and effective.

Although we focus on customer-valued processes, we mentioned throughout the book that there are customers for every process because there are both internal and external customers. Internal customers receive output from another internal organization or process. One type of internal customers is the business units supported by the functions. The processes of the support functions feed into the enterprise-wide business processes. If there are defects in the processes of the functions, there will be defects in the enterprise-wide business processes. Another type of internal customer is the next step in the sequence of a process. Each step of a process is executed with or without defects. If the step has a defect, that defect is passed on to the next step and eventually to the output of the process. This output becomes the input of another process. As defects accumulate throughout the processes, it becomes harder and harder to control the final output to the end customer or consumer. That is why a key aspect of CI is to reduce unnecessary work and variation in a process. The fewer activities performed in a process, the less variation that can occur.

Also note the word "continually" in the description. Your CI program never stops looking for more efficient and effective ways to do something. Creating the mentality that CI is part of every employee's job is critical for this type of program to work long term.

164

But it starts with the CEO. CEO commitment is vital for the rest of the organization to follow suit. This restructuring effort is the one thing a CEO can leave as a legacy that will help the company for years to come, even after he or she is gone. The determination to build the metrics, organization, and skills to carry on the improvement methodology long after the CEO has left is a valuable asset to leave behind. The CEO needs to make sure that continuous improvement is linked to the company's core values as well as to compensation. During your strategy session, build a mission and value statement that contains the improvement mind-set as a cultural attribute. Make employees understand that always looking for ways to improve processes and activities is something the company values and that will drive and reinforce the right behaviors. The goal should be to empower the workforce by using the disciplined approach of Six Sigma, Lean, and Theory of Constraints. Because decisions will be made using facts, data, and analysis, employees make recommendations to management that are statistically sound,

---

Quick Tip

☞ Communicate a "win" of the month on the company website or in a blast e-mail from the CEO. This will act as a nonmonetary reward . . . and everyone likes to be acknowledged for a job well done. Remember all the change management and communication messages we talked about in Chapter 5—Burning Platform, Elevator Speech, CEO and SLT monthly communications? Well, they are still used. The frequency stays the same, only now we move from "changing" the business model to "improving" the business model. The same pattern continues, with a communication plan highlighting the status of the projects and the wins the team and business achieve by implementing the tools and processes of CI.

with rationales supported by data from an accurate data model. (I hope you followed the advice in the beginning of the book and set up your data model correctly.) The fact that they present their own recommendations breeds confidence in the employees, and will transcend any fear they may have felt prior to being trained in Six Sigma and CI.

CI Organization Structure and Roles

What role does the CI team play in embedding a CI thought process into the organization?

- Those on the Continuous Improvement team are dedicated to fixing and tracking broken processes.
- They build the communication plan that constantly shows the wins and value from CI.
- They manage the metrics in the balanced scorecard that are linked to CI.

Let us talk about the organization that is needed for long-term success. You must have a CI organization and the leader must report to the CEO . . . period! Pushing it down in the organization is a big mistake. If your CI organization reports into anyone else, it will be suboptimal. The CEO needs to know the pulse of the organization and how his or her company is functioning. Having the CI organization report to the CEO shows employees that the CEO means business and CI is important. This does not mean, however, that meetings to review metrics should bog down the CEO.

How the projects are reviewed is something completely different. It is done through a CI Council, which is usually made up of the CEO, CFO, CIO, and all the operating leaders, plus the previous Steering Committee. Projects are reviewed at a high level using a dashboard, funding is discussed for improvements using a standard return on investment (ROI) model, as with new technology systems, and new projects are prioritized according to the strategy and impact to the business. The CI Council should meet biweekly at a minimum and can be part of the CEO SLT meetings. If you are executing projects that impact the business dramatically, you may need to meet more often. The reviews should only take an hour because they are merely updates to the last review. The leader of the CI organization is responsible for tracking and reviewing these items with the CI Council.

As discussed in Chapter 3, we recommend using project management software to keep track of all your projects. This may initially require a part-time resource in the CI organization to set up the database and create rules for everyone using the database (e.g., project name). Once everyone in the CI organization is trained on the software and the rules, entering the projects becomes part of their day-to-day job responsibility. Reports can be customized to provide the CI Leader with daily, weekly, or monthly metrics as well as special requests that may be needed only once. A report for the CI Council meetings includes only four important items:

1. **Status of project.** This is a one-sentence summary indicating what the issue is that is being solved, how it is being fixed, and by what organization. Metrics related to the project should be reviewed as well to see progress.
2. **Issues and roadblocks.** This section lists any issue or roadblock that needs the help from someone on the CI council or a decision that needs to be made by the entire CI council.
3. **Funding and cost/benefit analysis.** This section lists any projects that require funds to fix the issue (i.e., system enhancement or additional resources) and the cost/benefit analysis that was performed. The appropriate finance leader of the organization requesting the funds must sign off here.
4. **Action item follow-up.** This section reviews any action items that were assigned at the last CI Council meeting and their status.

Now let us look at the resources that make up the CI organization and the process for managing this organization. Before you create a CI organization, first you must hire the CI Leader. This person must have a Continuous Improvement background and be a certified Six Sigma Master Black Belt or Black Belt. He or she should have extensive experience managing multiple projects and large, dispersed teams, have finance acumen, and be a great communicator. As this person will lead by example, he or she must have executive presence and be an excellent speaker. *Do not* just throw anyone into this job or use it as a promotion, especially someone whose job has been eliminated but you want to keep in the company. Nine times out of ten you will have to find this person from outside your company using a headhunter, especially if you do not have a CI organization or you have only a few people in the company doing continuous improvement. Finding the right person for this job is worth the expense; it will make the entire SLT's jobs easier and ensure long-term success.

Quick Tip

☞ Hire a headhunter when you start your restructuring project and search for a person from a company that is well known for its Six Sigma program. Such a person will be able to hit the ground running and transition the restructuring organizational structure into the CI organizational structure when the project is winding down.

The CI Leader needs to have a strict pattern of weekly CI reviews with the entire team to keep abreast of issues and best practices. These meetings are typically half-day events with approximately 50 projects reviewed. Organizations with more projects than that may want to consider grouping the projects and rotating the reviews so each group is reviewed only once or twice a month.

A standardized, status report similar to the one used by the CI Council is ideal for the project reviews, but with more detail regarding the issue and how it is being solved. Typically a couple of Six Sigma tools are used to show the group how the root cause was determined. Each project presentation to the CI organization should take only five minutes. This is also a great opportunity for the people who lead the projects to get exposure to a senior-level person.

Once you find the CI Leader it is time to fill the director/ project manager positions. These people will have responsibility for processes as defined by the American Productivity and Quality Center (APQC) Process Classification Framework^{SM} (PCF). The most beneficial structure breaks the PCF into three distinct parts from the end customer's point of view: They are Inquiry to Order, Order to Cash, and Management/Support. Exhibit 8.2 defines these processes. We recommend having three directors/project managers, each responsible for several categories. One director would be responsible for all the PCF processes that make up the inquiry to order process, which would include PCF categories 1.0, 2.0, and 3.0. The second director would be responsible for all the PCF processes that make up the order to cash process, which would include PCF categories 4.0 and 5.0. The third director would be responsible for all the management and support processes that make up the APQC PCF. The support functions include finance, human resources, legal, and so forth, and are PCF categories 6.0 to 12.0. These directors should be Six Sigma Master Black Belts and also be familiar with Lean and Kaizen. They must have previous project management experience. Good candidates for these roles are the CI Champions who led the BPI processes during the restructuring effort.

The main responsibility of these directors is to review each project in their area and mentor the people working for them on the process and tools for Continuous Improvement. They should have weekly reviews with their team and daily reviews with those

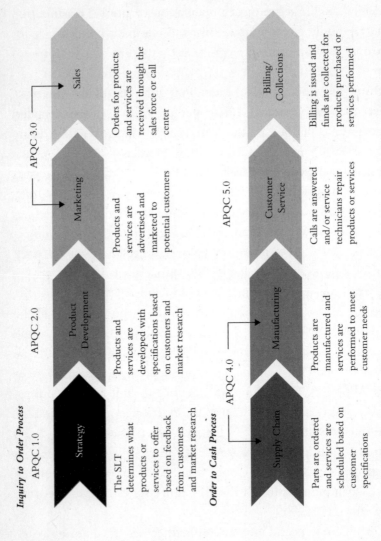

Inquiry to Order Process

APQC 1.0   APQC 2.0   APQC 3.0

Strategy

The SLT determines what products or services to offer based on feedback from customers and market research

Product Development

Products and services are developed with specifications based on customers and market research

Marketing

Products and services are advertised and marketed to potential customers

Sales

Orders for products and services are received through the sales force or call center

Order to Cash Process

APQC 4.0   APQC 5.0

Supply Chain

Parts are ordered and services are scheduled based on customer specifications

Manufacturing

Products are manufactured and services are performed to meet customer needs

Customer Service

Calls are answered and/or service technicians repair products or services

Billing/ Collections

Billing is issued and funds are collected for products purchased or services performed

Exhibit 8.2 APQC Process Classification Framework[SM] and Business Operations Alignment

170

who are deep in the analysis phase of their project. They should be asking "Why?" often enough that they are satisfied that the root cause has been found, in order to ensure that the tools are being used correctly.

Under the directors/project managers is a pooled organization of continuous improvement personnel. They do not all have to be Six Sigma Black Belts, but they should be Green Belts at a minimum, working toward their Black Belts. Having the entire organization understand the Six Sigma methodology and tools is essential to continuity. Good candidates for these roles are the Program Managers who ran the Level 2 processes during the restructuring effort. These are not entry-level positions. Many of these people will be leading several projects, so they need to have good analytical abilities, be great at team dynamics, and be very organized.

Projects are assigned to the pooled personnel based on the prioritization from the CI Council and the availability of Black/Green Belts. The CI Leader makes the final determination as to who leads a particular project, grouping projects in the same process together under the same person. One person should be able to handle 6 to 10 projects at a time, depending on experience and ability. These are the only full-time employees on the project, because the other team members already have full-time jobs. If there are too many projects for one person to handle, the CI Leader may distribute the projects and give them to several people. It is critical for these people to share findings and best practices not only during the weekly CI reviews but also on an ad hoc basis. Exhibit 8.3 depicts the optimal CI organization and the inquiry to order and order to cash processes respectively.

CI Dashboard

So far, we have talked at length about the rigor required to manage the changes and improve your business processes. But what

171

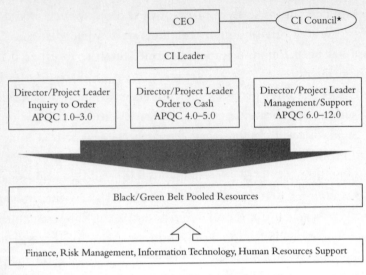

Exhibit 8.3 Continuous Improvement Organization

mechanism makes this all possible? The answer is a dashboard, either a CI dashboard or business performance management dashboard. You can call it what you like, but I like to call it a CI dashboard, because many people use the term "BPM" in different ways, and I do not want to confuse you.

The CI dashboard tracks the metrics of the processes and assigns a rating based on how close it is to the acceptable quality level (AQL). The ideal AQL is zero defects. Any acceptance of something other than zero is a compromise, although, in reality, it is based on acceptable business, financial, and safety levels and the agreement of internal and external customers to such levels.

In order to set up the CI dashboard, you will three data items for each subprocess:

1. Benchmarks
2. Baselines
3. AQLs

Basically, the dashboard is a simple way to measure the performance of your business processes against your own, those of your competitors, and what your customers want.

You should already have the benchmarks from the assessment stage. Now this information will be used as an improvement tool to measure your performance or process against other companies' best practices. You will use the information to improve your performance by establishing the benchmarks as the goals for your organization to reach.

Baselining is the process where you assess the quality and cost effectiveness of a process you are performing currently, so you can track improvements and progress as you implement changes to the process. The term "baselining" is used to compare yourself against yourself; "benchmarking" is used when you compare yourself against other companies.

The final input into the CI dashboard are the AQLs. The customers are both internal and external, and they define what they are willing to accept in the way of defects to any given process. The AQLs establish the key performance indicators (KPIs) that will be used in performance management. So, for example, if I am an apparel manufacturer, I may track defects per garment as one of my supply chain subprocess KPIs. The defects can come from many sources: defects in the fabric rolls, poor sewing, improper handling and packaging, and so on. If I am the supply chain process owner and my customer—the stores—agreed to only 1 out of 10 garments to be defective, and I am shipping 3 of 10 garments with defects, I need to figure out the root cause and improve the process. The AQL is 1 in this example.

Once you have accumulated the benchmarks, baselines, and AQLs for your subprocesses, you can build your dashboard, which will be reviewed with the CEO and CI organization.

It may look something like Exhibit 8.4.

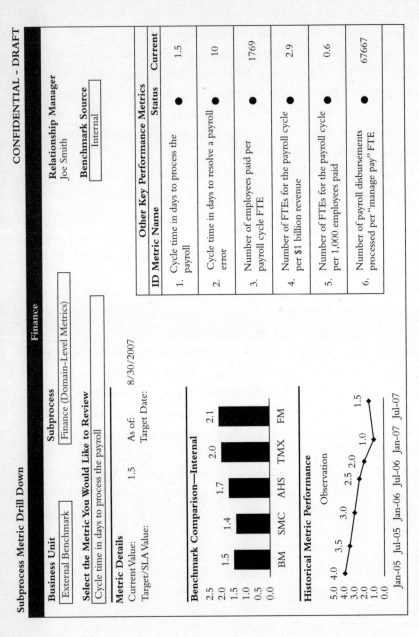

Subprocess Metric Drill Down

Finance

Business Unit	**Subprocess**		**Relationship Manager**
External Benchmark	Finance (Domain-Level Metrics)		Joe Smith

Select the Metric You Would Like to Review

Cycle time in days to process the payroll

			Benchmark Source
			Internal

Metric Details

Current Value: 1.5 As of: 8/30/2007
Target/SLA Value: Target Date:

Other Key Performance Metrics

ID	Metric Name	Status	Current
1.	Cycle time in days to process the payroll	●	1.5
2.	Cycle time in days to resolve a payroll error	●	10
3.	Number of employees paid per payroll cycle FTE	●	1769
4.	Number of FTEs for the payroll cycle per $1 billion revenue	●	2.9
5.	Number of FTEs for the payroll cycle per 1,000 employees paid	●	0.6
6.	Number of payroll disbursements processed per "manage pay" FTE	●	67667

Benchmark Comparison—Internal

2.5
2.0   1.5   1.4   1.7   2.0   2.1
1.5
1.0
0.5
0.0
BM   SMC   AHS   TMX   FM

Historical Metric Performance

Observation

5.0   4.0
4.0   3.5
3.0   3.0   2.5   2.0
2.0   1.0   1.5
1.0
0.0
Jan-05 Jul-05 Jan-06 Jul-06 Jan-07 Jul-07

Exhibit 8.4 Continuous Improvement Dashboard Governance Tool

Training

Training the organization on the process and tools used to implement a restructuring plan will be essential to creating a continuous improvement mind-set. Employees need to understand the language and methodology, but more so, they need to use it over and over in their daily activities to create value for the business.

Each stakeholder group requires its own training. For example, the CEO and SLT may need to understand only the general terminology and tools so they can ask the right questions to the CI organization and business units. However, the CI organization and process owners will need to be certified as Black Belts or Master Black Belts, if possible. And then there are all the employees who live the processes every day. They need to have an understanding of what CI is and how to implement it on their own, without the need of extensive classroom instruction or certification.

The CEO and SLT undergo executive CI training. It can last three days or up to one week, depending on the level of detail in the class. This training should be delivered through an external instructor, and the information should give the audience enough knowledge to make them dangerous.

We already discussed the training for the CI organization and the process owners: They must be certified. You can bring in an external instructor or send them to a class off-site.

Quick Tip

☞ Six Sigma training companies can provide you with online and off-site classroom training opportunities. They will also let you post jobs so you can fill your CI organization with professionals who are already trained.

As for the rest of the employees, below is an example of what my sister, Paula Zilka Colbert, BPI Practice leader at my firm, did while at GE as Quality leader and Master Black Belt for the corporate benefits organization. The corporate benefits organization was essentially a large COE with several large suppliers that provided services through processing and call centers for GE's various benefits programs. The supplier's employees may or may not be college educated, so the goal was to create a process training program that all employees could understand and relate to, with concepts and tools that they could use in their daily routines.

She decided to use the example of a fast-food drive-thru to simulate a process. It was broken down into steps that everyone could understand. Since it is a common experience for many people, it was very easy for the group to put themselves in the role of the customer and consider what they would expect out of their drive-thru experience. This is the most critical part of the process for them to understand; everything else is based on understanding those needs. Once the group determined the needs, they identified common issues that occur when one goes through a drive-thru. Although the example had already been created for the group, she took a few minutes to brainstorm some other issues that they may have experienced. It is important to talk about how often an issue could occur and if it is really something that needs to be captured, so the group does not get bogged down on issues that occur only rarely. Next the group moves on to the potential causes of an issue. Again, it is good to get the group brainstorming even though the example already lists the most likely causes. Finally they looked at potential improvements. Some may require analysis, but we are talking about people who may or may not know how to perform detailed analysis, so it is critical for them to think about what they would do to improve the issues. They may not be right, but at least they are starting to grasp process improvement. They will feel empowered, assessing the activities they perform on a day-to-day basis, naturally looking to make improvements. Exhibit 8.5 is an example to which most people can

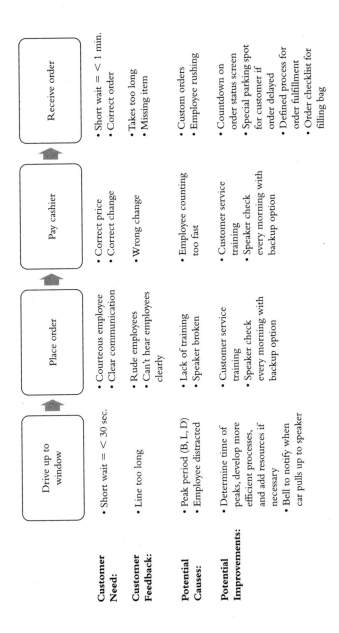

	Drive up to window	Place order	Pay cashier	Receive order
Customer Need:	• Short wait = < 30 sec.	• Courteous employee • Clear communication	• Correct price • Correct change	• Short wait = < 1 min. • Correct order
Customer Feedback:	• Line too long	• Rude employees • Can't hear employees clearly	• Wrong change	• Takes too long • Missing item
Potential Causes:	• Peak period (B, L, D) • Employee distracted	• Lack of training • Speaker broken	• Employee counting too fast	• Custom orders • Employee rushing
Potential Improvements:	• Determine time of peaks, develop more efficient processes, and add resources if necessary • Bell to notify when car pulls up to speaker	• Customer service training • Speaker check every morning with backup option	• Customer service training • Speaker check every morning with backup option	• Countdown on order status screen • Special parking spot for customer if order delayed • Defined process for order fulfillment • Order checklist for filling bag

Exhibit 8.5 Process Training for Large Groups

177

relate: going through a drive-thru window. It does not necessarily include 100 percent of the needs, issues, causes, or improvements, but it doesn't need to. It is intended to get large organizations to think in a process mind-set and feel empowered to make improvements in the processes that make up their job responsibilities on a daily basis.

Knowledge Management

The fourth and final piece to sustaining and continuously improving your business comes from managing the knowledge inherent in the organization. Companies have different definitions for knowledge management (KM), but I use this one:

> KM efforts typically focus on organizational objectives such as improved performance, competitive advantage, innovation, the sharing of lessons learned, and continuous improvement of the organization. KM efforts overlap with Organizational Learning, and may be distinguished from that by a greater focus on the management of knowledge as a strategic asset and a focus on encouraging the sharing of knowledge. KM efforts can help individuals and groups to share valuable organizational insights, to reduce redundant work, to avoid reinventing the wheel per se, to reduce training time for new employees, to retain intellectual capital as employees turnover in an organization, and to adapt to changing environments and markets.[1]

Several types of knowledge need to be captured in a knowledge management database:

- **Tribal knowledge.** Unwritten information to execute processes that is not commonly known by others within a company; sometimes it entails going around the process.
- **Technical/SME knowledge.** Expertise in performing a specialized job, task, or skill. The SME is the go-to person within the organization.

- **Process knowledge.** Expertise in designing, sustaining, and identifying future improvement opportunities in the process.

Most companies' knowledge reside in the experiences of long-tenured employees, information that is not necessarily available because it is in the minds of the people doing the work. This tribal knowledge is important for the company to capture and maintain in its knowledge management system. The best way to manage the knowledge is to use a technology solution that allows the three different sources to upload new information on their own. You should identify someone in the IT department to work on the solution and be responsible for quarterly updates to the system. As discussed earlier, it is important to invest in the system because it will allow for cross-enterprise knowledge sharing and helps your company become more efficient.

Linkages to CI

The final step to ensure that you are constantly improving your business is to link the CI organization with other business functions. There should be biweekly meetings with finance, risk management, human resources, and IT to ensure that they are aware of the improvements and projects coming down the pike. In most cases, their functions will be required to help implement the changes. The CI organization is responsible for keeping open, flowing communications among the functions. Additionally, each team should have at least one person who is Six Sigma certified and be responsible for driving improvements by partnering with the CI organization. These functional resources are not part of the CI organization but may participate on CI project leader teams. Additionally, their role is to improve processes of their functions using the standard methodology and tools provided by the CI organization.

The strength of the linkage between the support functions and the CI organization will determine the speed of execution of the improvements, so do not underestimate its significance.

Take the time to ensure that there is no duplication of efforts in your business. During one restructuring assignment my firm worked on, the organization seemed to be in complete chaos with cost cutting initiatives, and I assumed the CEO was aware. It appeared as though he had no control over the business unit leaders, because he was focused on the customers, while his leaders were all working on initiatives independently and not communicating to each other. When we started the project, the PMO began listing all the projects currently being worked on, so we could understand where there were synergies with the formal restructuring project to gain leverage on resources, tools, and standard methodologies. It took months just to get the lists together, but when we did and identified the ones that the restructuring team should take over, there was huge pushback from the leaders. When we went to the CEO for support, the CEO said, "I don't want to stop what they are doing." The problem was, they were taking three times as long to do it, they were not using the right financial or statistical measurements, and, basically, they were not looking at the whole process, just a piece, so there were huge holes in processes and were not being addressed. Merging the projects seemed like a no-brainer, but resistance can overpower logic.

We ended up duplicating a lot of what the company already was doing in the business unit because we were looking at the processes enterprise wide. What a waste of money and effort because the CEO there was not strong enough to say "Focus on your core business, and let the restructuring experts fix the problems that you hired them to fix."

Note

1. Mark P. A. Thompson and Geoff Walsham "Placing Knowledge Management in Context," *Journal of Management Studies* 41, no. 5 (2004): 725–747.

Chapter 9

Summary of Lessons Learned

It always amazes me to look back on a project and see how much the people have learned and grown. Not just in the skills they have acquired, but also in the confidence that understanding a complex process like restructuring provides. So I thought it would be a good idea to take a look back at the key lessons learned from the restructuring process I outlined for you and your team.

Chapter 1: Defining where you are on the "Conscious/ Unconscious" Continuum using the 10-minute checklist. As the first step, it is a reality check and may come as a surprise, but do not let it deter you. As with anything that needs to be fixed, admitting you have issues with your business and taking action is the first step.

Chapter 2: Understanding the framework, road map, and play-book to execute a restructuring project. Here you identify the foundational pieces of the project, such as data, finance, change management, and communications that will support the workstreams and ultimately make it easier to conduct business. Although some leaders try to do this by implementing short-term cost-cutting tactics, we laid out how each workstream delivers short-, mid-, or long-term opportunities.

Chapter 3: Building the project team, tools, and processes required to put the playbook into action. We define roles and responsibilities as well as the type of skills required to take on a role in a restructuring project. Having the right people in the right job is essential when you are changing the way your company operates.

Chapter 4: Identifying the right metrics to track to truly understand your company's performance, starting with your strategy road map. The link between your strategy road map and your balanced scorecard is imperative to reaching your financial and operational goals, yet so many companies fall short of ever making the connection. We describe how to build and link both tools so the entire organization can understand them. The self-assessment in the chapter tells the truth about where your company stands.

Chapter 5: Specifying the agenda items and documents for you to cover for a successful launch. Most important, we address the change management and communication issues, and how important it is to position the restructuring project correctly.

Chapter 6: Dealing with details. The devil is in the details and this chapter reviews each workstream's tools and processes plus case studies. We take you through how my firm and I execute our framework and the importance of managing workstream interdependencies.

Chapter 7: Identifying leaders. Leadership is essential to the success of any endeavor. Identifying the right people for the right jobs to lead a project is not an easy task. Today, it is more than just what is on their resume or last performance appraisal. People are born with certain natural skills, and the chapter reviews how to identify people's inherent talents to build the right team to execute the restructuring project successfully.

Chapter 8: Sustaining your improvements. Sustaining the improvements you made to your business will be the key to reducing your costs and increasing your profits. To do so, it is necessary to build the right organization to ensure you are continuously improving. This is where most companies fail. They make the changes but do not continue using the methodologies and tools they employed during the restructuring project. We suggest an organizational model and dashboard you can implement so you stay ahead of your competitors.

As companies mature and technologies and methodologies advance, the way we conduct business evolves too. What was common 10 years ago is no longer appropriate, so companies must improve continually in order to cut costs and increase profit. Restructuring is one of the methods that will help position a company for the future. Progressive concepts identified in restructuring have already become the norm in some companies. Exhibit 9.1

What's In	What's Out
CEOs "own" restructuring	CFOs "own" restructuring
Empowered employees	Bureaucracy and hierarchy
Innovation starting from the bottom up	Ideas driven from the top down
Facts, data, and analysis decision making	Intuitive analysis decision making
Investing in technology and productivity tools	Cutting IT budget to make the qtr/yr
Long-term strategic thinking	Short-term cost-cutting mentality
Transparency: Open and honest communication to employees	Elite communication: Only the leaders know the real story
Leaders managing a remote workforce	People working together in same building
Companies focusing on core business and outsourcing noncore activities	Companies who manage everything in-house

Exhibit 9.1 What Is In and What Is Out

depicts concepts identified as lessons learned by companies that my firm and I have consulted with.

I hope this book has provided you with the approach and tools to enable you to move to from "Unconscious Incompetence" to "Unconscious Competence." Ultimately, you should be running your company efficiently and effectively, and by now you should have seen the results of your efforts. Your cost model should be flexible, with levers you can pull depending on the industry and market conditions. Your organization should be lean and sharp, and able to expand and contract based on business needs. Your processes should be streamlined and automated and moving toward benchmark standards. You should have strong partnerships with vendors and suppliers that can provide you with the services to execute noncore, non–value-added processes. And best of all, your profit should be increasing as your costs are decreasing, allowing you to withstand any economic conditions.

If you have not already begun the journey of restructuring, it is not too late. Just be realistic about how long it will take to see results. Restructuring is a complicated process. If done correctly, it will take time, so be patient. As a leader, the best thing you can do when you leave or retire is to depart with a strong legacy and a reputation for making the company a better place, both financially and operationally. And is that not the name of the game?

Glossary

Term	Definition
Action Register	An action register is used to track and manage all actions identified for an initiative, project or program. Key details include a description of the action required, date the action was identified, date the action is required to be completed by, the primary person responsible for the action and the current status.
At the Customer, For the Customer (ACFC)	Customer based tool focused on the end needs of customer. Those needs are translated into actionable items the company can take to meet those needs.

Term	Definition
Balanced Scorecard	A strategic performance management tool for measuring whether the smaller-scale operational activities of a company are aligned with its larger-scale objectives in terms of vision and strategy.
Benchmarking	The process of comparing the cost, cycle time, productivity, or quality of a specific process or method to another that is widely considered to be an industry standard or best practice.
Best in Class (BIC)	Highest current performance level in an industry, used as a standard or benchmark to be equaled or exceeded.
Burning Platform	A statement from the CEO explaining "why" the restructuring program is necessary and how important it is to the business.
Business Continuity Plan	A defined plan of action that allows the business to continue normal operations in light of all possible events. A Business Continuity Plan is especially crucial during times of transformation and change to ensure a positive customer experience.
Business Core Competency Model (BCCM)	A tool developed by NexGen to visually depict where a particular process falls within Shared Services, Center of Excellnce, and CORE activities.

Term	Definition
Business Intelligence	Refers to skills, technologies, applications and practices used to help a business acquire a better understanding of its commercial context.
Business Process Improvement (BPI)	A systematic approach to help any organization optimize its underlying processes to achieve more efficient results through various vehicles including Six Sigma, Lean, Theory of Constraints, Kaizen, etc.
Business Process Management (BPM)	a field of management focused on aligning organizations with the wants and needs of clients. It is a holistic management approach[1] that promotes business effectiveness and efficiency while striving for innovation, flexibility, and integration with technology.
Business Process Outsourcing (BPO)	Business Process Outsourcing is the act of giving a third-party the responsibility of running what would otherwise be an internal system or service.
Business Process Re-Engineering (BPR)	A management technique used to improve the efficiency and effectiveness of business processes.
Centers of Excellence (COE)	Organizations that translates units strategy into best-in-class tactical plans and procedures and prioritize activities to deliver on strategy execution.
Champion	A member of the restructuring project's Steering Committee.

Term	Definition
Change Management	A structured approach to transitioning individuals, teams, and organizations from a current state to a desired future state. The current definition of change management includes both organizational change management processes and individual change management models, which together are used to manage the people side of change.
Continuous Improvement	A management process whereby delivery (customer valued) processes are constantly evaluated and improved in the light of their efficiency, effectiveness and flexibility
Control Phase	The final element of the DMAIC process. Control phase ensures that any deviations from target are corrected before they result in defects.
Core	Refers to those activities or processes that are truly critical to the enterprise. Core activities are often strategic in nature and the health, performance and maturity of these processes are central to the company's overall performance.
Customer Retention	A company's ability to attract and retain new customers.
delayering	a term in management and corporate restructuring that refers to a planned reduction in the number of layers of a organizational hierarchy.

Term	Definition
DMAIC	A structured problem-solving methodology widely used in business and Six Sigma. The acronym stands for Define, Measure, Analyze, Improve and Control. The term is pronounced "Duh-MAY-ick"
Drill Down Tree	Tool used in Six Sigma to aid in peeling back the onion so root cause or $Y=f(x)$ variables can be found.
Elevator Speech	Short, concise paragraph outlining what the program is about and how you will go about achieving the goals you've set.
Enterprise Resource Planning (ERP)	A company-wide computer software system used to manage and coordinate all the resources, information, and functions of a business from shared data stores.
Facilitation	The act of leading a company and its employees through Work-Out sessions and the various other elements of the restructuring effort.
Failure Modes and Effects Analysis (FMEA)	A procedure for analysis of potential failure modes within a system for classification by severity or determination of the effect of failures on the system.
Fishbone diagrams	Tool used in Six Sigma that categorizes issues into several categories (bones). Brainstorming or analysis is then performed to find the root cause issues causing the problem. Issues are smaller bones extending from the larger bones (categories).

Term	Definition
Forming-Storming-Norming-Performing	A model of group development that was first proposed by Bruce Tuckman in 1965, who maintained that these phases are all necessary and inevitable in order for the team to grow, to face up to challenges, to tackle problems, to find solutions, to plan work, and to deliver results.
Framework	A basic conceptual structure used to solve or address complex issues.
Full Time Equivalent (FTE)	An FTE of 1.0 means that the person is equivalent to a full-time worker, while an FTE of 0.5 signals that the worker is only half-time.
Functional Core Competency Model	Tool used to identify opportunities to 1. Eliminate 2. Optimize 3. Outsource 4. Improve/Outsource Business Processes.
Governance	Governance relates to decisions that define expectations, grant power, or verify performance. It consists either of a separate process or of a specific part of management or leadership processes.
Hackett	The Hackett Group is a global strategic advisory firm specializing in best practice advisory, benchmarking, and transformation consulting services, including shared services, offshoring and outsourcing advice.
human capital	The stock of skills and knowledge embodied in the ability to perform labor so as to produce economic value.

Term	Definition
Information Technology Outsourcing (ITO)	Information Technology Outsourcing is identical to BPO, but refers to activities within the IT domain only.
Inquiry to Order (ITO)	The first part of a company's lifecycle process. Begins at the point an inquiry about the product or service is made by the potential customer to the company through a phone call, email request, online, etc., to the point where an order is placed by the customer.
International Organization for Standardization (ISO)	an international-standard-setting body composed of representatives from various national standards organizations. Founded on 23 February 1947, the organization promulgates worldwide proprietary industrial and commercial standards.
key performance indicator (KPI)	Financial and non-financial measures or metrics used to help an organization define and evaluate how successful it is, typically in terms of making progress towards its long-term organizational goals.
Knowledge Database	A central repository that houses all of the critical information regarding business processes. Information stored in the knowledge database includes cost, staffing, process maps, key performance indicators, SLAs and organizational charts.

Term	Definition
knowledge management	A range of practices used in an organisation to identify, create, represent, distribute and enable adoption of insights and experiences. Such insights and experiences comprise knowledge, either embodied in individuals or embedded in organisational processes or practice.
layers	Refers to the various reporting levels that exist within an organization.
Lean	a production practice that considers the expenditure of resources for any goal other than the creation of value for the end customer to be wasteful, and thus a target for elimination.
Level 2 Processes	High-level divisions of the various process categories within the APQC process efficiency framework.
milestones	Progress markers inserted thoughout the project's timeline to signify the completion of a significant event or series of events related to the realization your project's end goal.
new product introductions (NPI),	term used to describe the complete process of bringing a new product or service to market.
Non-Core	Refers to those activities or processes that, while essential to the company's functionality, do not define the business. Non-Core processes are often common across industries and generally do not serve as competitive differentiators.

Term	Definition
operational restructuring	The act of cutting fat from, reorganizing, and improving company processes, policies, and procedures.
Order to Cash (OTC)	The second half of a company's lifecycle process. Begins at the point the order is placed by the customer, through the manufacturing process to the end of the process where monies are collected for the product or service performed.
Organization diagnostic assessment (ODA),	An ODA comprises looking at the structure and metrics that provide the answers to how effi cient the organization is and what gaps exist to getting to benchmark.
Organizational Efficiency (OE),	One of three main workstreams in the business restructuring effort. Focuses on creating most cost effective and lean organizational design for a given company.
Pareto Charts	A bar chart that displays by frequency, in descending order, the most important defects. Proper use of this chart will have the cumulative percentage on a second y-axis (to the right of the chart).
Playbook	A scheme or set of strategies for conducting business.

Term	Definition
Term	**Definition**
PMO (project management office),	The Project Management Office (PMO) in a business or professional enterprise is the department or group that defines and maintains the standards of process, generally related to project management, within the organization. The PMO strives to standardize and introduce economies of repetition in the execution of projects.
Pulse Survey	A pulse survey is a powerful type of survey used to monitor the internal operating health, or climate, of the organisation.
RASCI model	A model used to help define who is responsible / accountable R: Responible A: Accountable S:Supportive C: Consulted I: Informed.
reductions in force (RIF)	The separation or downgrading of employees as a result of reorganization, lack of work, or a shortage of funds. A RIF is generally expressed as a percentage of an organization's work force.
Request for Proposal (RFP)	A document that is sent to outsourcing service providers that details the services the company is offering as potential candidates for outsourcing. The decision to outsource a given service is still uncertain at this point.
ROI Threshold	% Return on Investment company must realize for go/no go decision on business cases for investment, programs, etc.

Term	Definition
root cause issues	An identified reason for the presence of a defect or problem. The most basic reason, which if eliminated, would prevent recurrence. The source or origin of an event.
Scope Model	The model used during the outsourcing process, in conjunction with the development of the RFP. The scope model clearly defines which services will be provided by which parties.
Service Level Agreements (SLA)	Contractual relationships that define the level of service to be provided to the client. SLAs also dictate the penalties when the Agreement Levels are not met. Note that clients can be internal or external.
SG&A	Selling, General and Administrative: Expenses consisting of the combined payroll costs (salaries, commissions, and travel expenses of executives, sales people and employees), and advertising expenses a company incurs.
Shared Service	Organizations that execute on tactical plans determined by core and COE. Group of highly specialized specialists in their field that will execute on the tactical plans.

Term	Definition
Skip-Level Meetings	This meeting is a type of structured interview. The general purpose is to give managers an opportunity to gather employees' thoughts about the organization and to learn of their satisfactions, dissatisfactions and recommendations for the future.
Span of Control (SoC),	a term originating in military organization theory, but now used more commonly in business management, particularly human resource management. Span of control refers to the number of subordinates a supervisor has.
Sponsor	The project sponsor is the executive who manages, administers, monitors, funds, and is responsible for the overall project delivery. The sponsor may be owner, financier, client . . . or their delegate.
Stakeholders Analysis	Stakeholder Analysis is a tool used to identify and enlist support from stakeholders. It provides a visual means of identifying stakeholder support so that you can develop an action plan for your project.
Steering Committee	A Steering Committee is a group of high-level stakeholders who are responsible for providing guidance on overall strategic direction. They are usually composed of the decision makers in a company.

Term	Definition
Term	**Definition**
Strategy Council	Strategy Council is charged with developing the Road map and strategies to support its priority recommendations and objectives.
Strategy Road map	Represents a guideline which is necessary to follow during the entire project. A program for future development indicating what will be developed and when.
Subject Matter Expert (SME),	The Subject Matter Expert is that individual who exhibits the highest level of expertise in performing a specialized job, task, or skill within the organization. An SME might also be a software engineer, a helpdesk support operative, an accounts manager, a scientific researcher: in short, anybody with in-depth knowledge of the subject you are attempting to document.
Transition Management	The process of managing change in an investor's investments. Transition Management typically relates to large institutional investors (or groups of investors) with large asset pools they manage on behalf of beneficiaries.
Workout (WO!)	Typically two to three day meeting with a group of workstream members to deliver pre-determined milestones.
Workstreams	A group of people executing specific tasks based on a framework.

Index

Index

Index

Index

request for proposal (RFP), 131–132
resistance, 3, 18, 72
Restructuring Lead, 20, 29, 32–34,
36, 45, 74–75, 90, 110, 163
Return on Investment (ROI), 45,
133, 166
revenue, 2, 107
increase in, 2, 107–108
Risk Management, 30, 35, 43, 63,
71, 74
database, 42
leader, 35–37, 44, 133
system, 44
team, 74
risks and mitigants, 35, 70–71,
104–105
form, *see forms*
Road Map, 50–54, 56, 69, 92–93,
100, 131, 181–182
Five common elements of, 50
root cause issues, 4, 5, 37, 107, 118,
121, 171, 173

sales, 15, 39, 56, 62–63
forecasting, 63
global sales organization, 107–108
Schweitzer, Albert, 152
scorecard, *see balanced scorecard*
self-assessment scorecard, *see
assessments*
Senior Leadership Team (SLT), 15,
19–20, 32, 58, 60, 65–67,
70–75, 80, 82, 85–87, 162,
165, 167–168, 175
Senior Vice President (SVP), 15, 90,
93, 100–101, 104–105, 107,
112, 114
SG&A (selling, general, and
administrative), 1, 135
as percentage of revenue, 6, 7
Shared Service, *see Business Core
Competency Model*

SIPOC Diagram, 111, 116, 118–119
Six Sigma, 23, 26, 33, 44–46, 65, 95,
108, 112, 116, 128, 162, 166,
168–169, 171, 179
Black Belt, 37, 46, 112, 121, 128,
168–169, 171
drill-down trees, 46
failure modes and effects analysis
(FMEA), 46
fishbone diagrams, 46, 95, 98, 107
Green Belt, 112, 171
Kaizen, 108, 169
Lean, 23, 26, 44, 64–65, 108, 128,
162, 169
Master Black Belt, 33, 46, 121,
128, 168–169, 175
pareto charts, 46, 95–97, 107
training, 110, 162, 171
skip-level meetings, 9, 85–86
span of control (SoC), 25, 59–62,
104, 107
delayering, 83, 108
sponsor, 19–20
stakeholders' analysis, 70–73, 80
standard platforms, 7, 9
status update, *see forms*
Steering Committee, 21, 29, 32, 36,
40, 45, 70, 79, 110, 128
strategic planning, 145
strategic positioning, 140
strategy, *see change management
communication*
Strategy Council, 10
resources for, 33
Subject Matter Expert (SME),
22–23, 62, 100, 108, 118, 120,
129, 178
Success Factors and Derailers, 27
supplier, 132–133
supply chain, 56, 63–64, 128
supply chain management
(SCM), 63